duffy. robbins

BUILDING A YOUTH MINISTRY THAT BUILDS DISCIPLES

A Small Book About a Big Idea

duffy robbins

BUILDING A YOUTH MINISTRY THAT BUILDS DISCIPLES

A Small Book About a Big Idea

youth specialties

ZONDERVAN.com/
AUTHORTRACKER
follow your favorite authors

ZONDERVAN

Building a Youth Ministry That Builds Disciples
Copyright © 2011 by Duffy Robbins

YS Youth Specialties is a trademark of YOUTHWORKS!, INCORPORATED and is registered with
the United States Patent and Trademark Office.

This title is also available as a Zondervan ebook.
Visit www.zondervan.com/ebooks.

Requests for information should be addressed to:

Zondervan, *Grand Rapids, Michigan* 49530

Library of Congress Cataloging-in-Publication Data

Robbins, Duffy.
    Building a youth ministry that builds disciples : a small book about a big idea / Duffy
Robbins.
       p. cm.
    Includes bibliographical references.
    ISBN 978-0-310-67030-8 (softcover)
    1. Church work with youth. 2. Church work with teenagers. 3. Discipling (Christianity) 4.
Christian youth—Religious life. 5. Christian teenagers—Religious life. I. Title.
BV4447.R625 2011
259'.23 — dc23   2011043946

Cover design: IMAGO
Interior design: David Conn

Printed in the United States of America

11 12 13 14 15 16 /DCI/ 23 22 21 20 19 18 17 16 15 14 13 12 11 10 9 8 7 6 5 4 3 2 1

This book is dedicated to two gifted (but *very different!*) leaders: Chuck Neder and Nate Parks. You don't know each other, but at the core you're very kindred spirits. You guys have made me laugh a lot, you've allowed me to work alongside you in co-ministry, you've inspired me by your faith, and you've been good friends who have enriched my life and my walk with Jesus. Thanks for everything!

And on behalf of the thousands of teenagers and youth workers who've been touched by your lives and ministries, thanks for what you do and who you are. I'm honored to dedicate this book to two of my youth ministry heroes.

"Therefore, my dear brothers and sisters, stand firm. Let nothing move you. Always give yourselves fully to the work of the Lord, because you know that your labor in the Lord is not in vain."

—1 Corinthians 15:58

CONTENTS

ACKNOWLEDGMENTS

Back in the mid-80s, a very kind woman named Liz Duckworth attended one of my seminars at a Youth Specialties convention in Chicago. When we met for coffee later that day, she explained that she was an acquisition editor for Victor Books and wondered if I might be able "to take that seminar we heard this morning and put it in the form of a book." That book, *Programming to Build Disciples* (1986), was the first one I ever wrote. To this day, I still get the occasional email or have a face-to-face conversation in which someone, somewhere, says, "That book really shaped my ministry."

Having written quite a few more books since then, I'm always encouraged to hear that God can take the water of typeset words and turn them into the wine of renewed youth ministry and changed lives. Because I've written a lot of books, people often say, "You must really love to write!" I don't—at least not when I'm sitting at my desk under the shadow of a deadline and thinking about 10 other ways I should or would like to use my time. But what I do like is *having written*. To be able to stand with amazing youth workers around the globe, to invest in their ministries and share their struggles is an amazing privilege and a precious honor.

It's a privilege I value in part because I can think of so many coworkers and friends who've played that role in my own life over the years: Whitney Alexander, Alan Ameye, George and Carol Anderson, Johnny "Dinger" Bell, Paul Borthwick, Murray Brown, Seth Buckley, David Burke, Jim Burns, Jim Byrnes, Tony Campolo, Chuck Chichowitz, Chap and Dee Clark, Bill Crofton, Jim Davis, Mark DeVries, Lanny and Peggy Donoho, Calenthia Dowdy, Ajith Fernando, Doug and Cathy Fields, Mike and Amy Flavin, Jack Gerry, Kami Gilmour, Mitch Gore, Chris and Debbie Hall, Mark Hallock, Barry Hill, Eric Keller, Crystal Kirgiss, Eric Kraihanzel, Dan and Cindy Kreiss, Danny Kwan, Tic and Terrie Long, Mark Matlock, Craig Mawhinney, Tiger McLuen, Joe and Marianne Modica, Walt and Lisa Mueller, Helen Musick, Nate Parks, Darrell Pearson, Marv and Lois Penner, Chuck and Susan Neder, Mark Oestreicher,

Dave Olshine, Eduardo Ramirez, Wayne and Marci Rice, Bob and Margaret Ann Seiple, Laurie Polich-Short, Dick Stanislaw, Roz Stirling (and the entire Presbyterian Church of Northern Ireland mafia—Barb, Graeme, Ruth, Lois, et. al.!), Nate Stratman, Bob and Pam Swan, Todd Temple, Harry Thomas, Vern Tyerman, Rich Van Pelt, James and Beth Ward, Ron Ward, J. L. and Patt Williams, Dave Wintsch, Mike and Karla Yaconelli, and hundreds more I haven't mentioned to whom I will certainly have to make apologies. Thanks to *all* of you for being my "cloud of witnesses." Your presence in my life has been a vivid demonstration of God's grace, goodness, and faithfulness. (And to the few remaining believers whose names were not on this list, tune in to my next book.)

The book you're holding in your hand (or reading from your cool electronic gadget) is an attempt to restate and rewrite some of the principles I initially discussed in that first book more than 25 years ago. The difference between now and then is that I've lived long enough to see some of the fruit that I only hoped for when I was younger, and I've learned hard lessons about some of the principles of ministry that were "crystal clear" when I was just starting out. But I trust this book will help a new generation of youth workers embrace the mandate of disciple-making in practical and inspiring ways.

Thanks to Doug Davidson, my editor. Once again, your suggestions, corrections, and mild rebukes have been invaluable. This is a much better book because of you, and lovers of gender-neutral pronouns everywhere owe you a debt of thanks!

Thanks again to sweet Maggie, my wife and best friend. Your companionship on this adventure is a delight, your pursuit of God is an inspiration, and your faithful love for your husband is a consistent demonstration of grace.

SECTION ONE
Design for Discipleship

CHAPTER 1
TARZAN
CHRISTIANITY

When I was a little boy, one of my favorite television heroes was Tarzan: King of the Jungle. My youthful imagination was stirred by the sight of this powerful man raised by animals in the thickest jungle. He slept in the mother of all tree houses, hundreds of feet above the jungle floor, and was always clad in his signature leopard-skin tankini. My favorite part of every show was when Tarzan—one part Superman, one part Samson, and one part Curious George on steroids—would grab a tree vine and swing from treetop to treetop as the whole jungle came alive with the sound of his trademark yell, which he did sometimes to communicate with the animals, and sometimes because the leopard-skin deal would get caught up in the vine.

It was an awesome image: Tarzan weaving his way from vine to vine, going bungee before bungee was cool. How amazing—and how convenient—that there was always a vine right where he needed it, one that was the right length and secure at the top yet somehow loose enough to release from the tree with the slightest tug.

Frankly, even as a young boy I used to wonder about that.

As I'd walk through the woods behind our house and look up at the treetops, I was certain it would take more than a quick pull to launch those vines. I wondered what might happen if Tarzan were swinging through the woods behind *my* house. First of all, I suspected he might get scuffed up a bit if he wore the leopard-skin outfit back there. There were some serious stickers. And he might get poison ivy on areas of his body that would make vine swinging more difficult—or at least less comfortable. But even more important, what about the vines? What if they weren't long enough, or what if they were too long? Plus, most of the vines behind my house were wrapped pretty securely around the trees—how would that affect my hero?

I imagined how sad it would be to see Tarzan swing down on a vine that was too long, only to crash to the jungle floor with a thud. Or what if he miscalculated and chose a vine that was too short? One can only imagine the blur of flailing flesh and leopard skin as Tarzan realizes Vine A won't allow him to swing to Tree B. Or how gruesome would it be if Tarzan were to swing all the way to the edge of the jungle and simply run out of trees? Imagine: Tarzan swings through the jungle...first to one tree...then another...then another...then another...until all of a sudden, he comes to a clearing. No trees. No vines. Just a small group of animals gawking at a "king" whose crown is seriously broken. Not a pretty thought.

And yet, it's precisely that thought that animates this book you're now holding.

WHAT IS THIS THING CALLED "YOUTH MINISTRY"—AND WHY DO WE DO IT?

When many of us think of youth ministry, we can almost imagine in our mind's eye a generation of teenagers "swinging" from Sunday night to Sunday night, youth meeting to youth meeting, coffee house to small group, Young Life club to Campaigner Camp, retreat to festival, summer camp to mission trip. We imagine great excitement in the air, an ever-growing number of students coming to youth group, and youth programs getting larger and gaining momentum.[1] In this grand vision, it would be easy to suppose that our job as club leaders, Sunday school teachers, and youth workers is simply to supply and supervise these treetop moments, to see that vines are loosed and ready, cut and cleared in neat lengths that maximize the ride. But, in fact, the greater task for those of us in youth ministry is to prepare our students for life in the clearing, for those times when the treetops give way and leave them feeling uncertain about what to grab onto. They must also be ready for those other times when the jungle of life gets too dense, when the excitement diminishes and the difficulty of finding the trail increases, when the Christian life becomes more about walking step to step than swinging from treetop to treetop.

This book is born of the concern that our current view of youth ministry leads us as leaders—paid and volunteer alike—to see ourselves as program planners, people who work with determination and creativity to create Disney-like jungle experiences that maximize the thrills and emphasize the treetops of the spiritual life. The problem with this contemporary approach to youth ministry is that it often breeds students who are ripe for a classic case of "crash and burn"—a plunging blur of leopard skin, colorful Bible cover, and Christian T-shirt.

If you're reading this book, it's probably because, like me, you love seeing teenagers grow up in their faith and mature into disciples who will follow Jesus faithfully throughout their lives. You've put up with bad food, loud music, loud human beings, late nights, awkward conversations, ungrateful parents, and countless other inconveniences precisely because you know, as I do, that growing teenagers into disciples is not just a possibility, but a unique and holy privilege. And, like me, I'll bet you've also discovered that it's a great adventure and a wild, fun ride. Because every now and then—in the midst of the bad food, loud music, loud human beings, late nights, awkward conversations, ungrateful parents, and countless other inconveniences—you get to see God.

But that's why I know you're concerned, as I am, because you're aware that when these students leave our youth groups, they won't always have the luxury of swinging from one treetop experience to the next. What will happen to them then? What will happen when they find themselves out there in the jungle of everyday life with all of its risks and dangers? Will their faith survive, or will it crash and burn in a blur of doubt, disillusion, and distraction?

I fear that in failing to ask such questions, we may be compromising God's mandate for the church and his call for those of us who serve him as youth workers. And, most of all, I'm concerned that in our discomfort with these kinds of questions, we may be planting in our youth programs the seeds of *Tarzan Christianity*.

IS THERE LIFE AFTER TREETOPS?

To be sure, it is God who begins the "good work" in the teenagers we work with, and it is God who will see it through to "completion"

(Philippians 1:6). But we youth workers must recognize that our task is not simply to get teenage Tarzans to jump into the jungle; we need to help them land, stand, and keep walking with Christ on a daily basis. The mission of effective youth ministry is not getting young people to "swing from the trees"; it's helping them cling to the Vine (John 15:5).

Any number of factors can short-circuit this important work. But ultimately, the key to preventing a nasty fall is maintaining a consistent balance in the way we do youth ministry—to recognize that we're not trying to build *swingers*, but *clingers*. Our mission is to build in students a faith that will last, a commitment that endures in the highest treetop moments and in the heart of the darkest jungle.

So let's begin with some diagnosis. What is it about so much of contemporary youth ministry that breeds Tarzan Christianity? What confusions about our own identity as youth workers keep us from understanding our role in this grace adventure? Where do we fall short in building long-term faith? What follows are some of the most common errors of imbalance.[2]

Imbalance 1: Too Much Arrival, Not Enough Survival

The Christian life is a marathon. It's never been about speed; it's always been about distance. It's not about how *fast* our young people grow; it's about how *far* our young people grow.

Let's be clear: *Arrival* is a very good thing. There's no greater satisfaction than being there when a young person you've been praying for, talking with, and walking with finally comes to that point where she wants to surrender her life to Christ. Who doesn't get excited about a birth announcement? Jesus said that even the angels rejoice when only one sinner repents (Luke 15:10). But nowhere in Scripture are we called to *make converts*; only God can *make converts*. Our mandate as youth workers is to *make disciples* (Matthew 28:19; 2 Timothy 2:2).

After all these years, I still haven't gotten over the wonder of seeing kids step forward (or say a prayer, or raise a hand, or make a decision, or quietly commit) to follow Christ. But at its core, our commission to make disciples means more than just leading kids to accept Christ as Savior. *Pressing onward* in the faith is more important than *coming forward* in a meeting. *Arrival* is good; *survival* is better.

Research from the Barna Group of Ventura, California, shows that most young people who show strong levels of spiritual activity during the teen years tend to pull back from active participation in the Christian faith during their young adult years. Sadly, many of them never return. Indeed, the Barna Group concludes that as many as 6 out of every 10 twentysomethings who were involved in a church during their teen years will fail to maintain their active spirituality during their years of emerging adulthood. "The research shows that, compared to older adults, twentysomethings have significantly lower levels of church attendance, time spent alone studying and reading the Bible, volunteering to help churches, donations to churches, Sunday school and small group involvement, and use of Christian media (including television, radio and magazines)."[3]

Perhaps the most troubling of these findings is that 61 percent of twentysomethings who'd been churched during their teen years are now spiritually disengaged (i.e., not actively attending church, reading the Bible, or praying). Only 20 percent of these young adults maintain a level of spiritual activity in their twenties that is consistent with their involvement in high school.[4] If this sounds a little grim, consider the results of the 2009 Pew Forum on Religion and Public Life, which prompted top political scientists Robert Putnam and David Campbell to comment, "Young Americans are dropping out of religion at an alarming rate of five to six times the historic rate (30 to 40 percent have no religion today, versus 5 to 10 percent a generation ago)."[5] These results correspond to Rainer Research studies that show about 70 percent of U.S. youth drop out of church between the ages of 18 and 22.[6]

Others suggest the picture isn't quite so dire.[7] Baylor University sociologist Rodney Stark contends, "Young people have always been less likely to attend [church] than are older people....A bit later in life when they have married, and especially after children arrive, they become more regular [church] attendees. This happens in every generation."[8] Indeed, Stark's conclusions are similar to those of another sociologist, Bradley Wright. In his book *Christians Are Hate-Filled Hypocrites...and Other Lies You've Been Told*, Wright remarks that the grave warning about young people leaving the church is nothing more than "one of the myths" of contemporary Christianity.[9] But all of us who love teenagers and care about nurturing in them a long-term commitment would agree that if we want to encourage in our students a faith that does not fail or fade, we need to focus on strategies that encourage survival, not just arrival.

That's not to say outreach is unimportant. Obviously, the church is called to give witness to Jesus (Acts 1:8). Those who pit "discipleship" against "evangelism" seem to have forgotten that evangelism is the first stage in the process of discipleship. No one has ever been discipled who was not first evangelized. Walk around the youth ministry neighborhood for a little while, and you'll probably meet folks who might be described as "discipleship snobs"—youth workers who talk about evangelism and outreach as if they were lower life-forms of youth ministry: "I don't have time to mess around with kids who aren't interested in doing something radical for Jesus! I didn't get into ministry so I could do fun and games." Fair enough. Most of us didn't. I understand that some kids are drawn to the deep. But about five minutes of immersion in adolescent culture demonstrates that many other teenagers are drawn to the shallow. And some of those kids *fear* the deep.

The value of fun and games, laser tag, lock-ins, crazy relays, stupid pet tricks, and Quidditch matches is that they provide us a context in which we can build relationships with teenagers. And like copper for electricity, relationships are the conductors through which we bring Light to kids living in darkness. We mustn't forget that discipleship happens in relationship, and relationships won't happen if we don't meet kids on their terms.

Standing on the beach one day, Jesus looked squarely into Peter's eyes and said, "Don't be afraid; from now on you will fish for people" (Luke 5:10). We can't be absolutely sure what Peter thought about that word picture. But we can be relatively sure that, as a fisherman, Peter knew it takes two things to catch fish: (1) patience, and (2) a net. Whether we like it or not, fishing for teenagers will always involve both. Fish don't report to the boat. It takes a lure. It takes bait. It takes a net.

Now, granted, some kids are self-aware enough to acknowledge the deep longings of their soul, thoughtful enough to consider their need for God, and honest enough to see beyond the blinders that our culture has placed on them. For these kids, a simple invitation to learn habits of prayer and communion may be all the bait it takes. To be sure, there is something powerfully attractive and deeply moving about the invitation to know God.

The problem is that ever since the garden (Genesis 3:8-9), human beings—particularly *adolescent* human beings—have demonstrated a profound ability to ignore those longings and hide from the very God whose invitation promises a place where hungers are fed, thirsts are quenched, and souls are satisfied (Isaiah 55:1-6; see also Romans 1:18-23).[10] There's a word for people in fishing boats who don't use nets or bait; they're called *passengers*. To do discipleship without evangelism is to do farming without sowing seeds. A wise farmer understands the importance of adding a little manure to the seed. A wise fisherman understands the importance of adding bait to the hook. (Deadliest Catch 3:16). And sometimes, for some teenagers, what smells like lightweight spiritual manure to those of us who want to go deeper is actually bait for those who are swimming in a very shallow culture.

Arrival is important. Nothing happens without arrival.

On the other hand, no fisherman in his right mind continues to catch fish without giving some thought to how he'll preserve them and keep them fresh. Otherwise, all he has to show for his labor at the end of the day is a big boat filled with smelly, dead fish. Big catch? Big deal.

The problem is that catching fish is more exhilarating than scaling them, cleaning them, and preserving them. Evangelism generates greater excitement and bigger numbers than discipleship and nurture do.

There is always more excitement in arrival than there is in survival. When guests first arrive at your home for a visit, there are hugs and kisses and animated conversations. Who wouldn't want to focus their efforts on that end of the equation? But after a few days of sharing the bathroom and cleaning up someone else's mess, we begin the mundane work of life in shared community. That's not quite as exhilarating.

So much of our youth ministry effort is focused on helping young people to "become Christians" that we've lost sight of our central

God-given mandate to build them into disciples, "baptizing them in the name of the Father and of the Son and of the Holy Spirit, and teaching them to obey everything I have commanded you" (Matthew 28:19-20). Surveys of church young people indicate that we're doing a better job of getting them to *show up* than helping them to *grow up*.

Commenting on Christian Smith's massive National Study on Youth and Religion (NSYR),[11] Kenda Creasy Dean puts it like this:

> We have successfully convinced teenagers that religious participation is for moral formation and for making nice people, which may explain why American adolescents harbor no ill will toward religion. Many of them say they will bring their own children to church in the future (a dubious prediction statistically). Yet these young people possess no real commitment to or excitement about religious faith. Teenagers tend to approach religious participation, like music and sports, as an extracurricular activity: a good well-rounded thing to do, but unnecessary for an integrated life.[12]

Our task in youth ministry is not just helping young people to become Christians; it's helping young people to *be* the Christians they've *become*. There is nothing wrong with cookouts, ski trips, movie nights, and bowling parties that draw big crowds. But when it's all said and done, we dare not focus so much on getting kids to arrive that we neglect the hard, less glamorous work of helping them survive.

Imbalance 2: Too Much Childish, Not Enough Childlike

It's too bad that real life is not a flannelgraph. It would be so much easier if we could reduce all of the hassles, temptations, and questions of life to a few cut-out felt figures. But real life doesn't always match the Sunday school simplicity of four or five figures clinging to a flannel background. Maybe it's our tendency to oversimplify that breeds an unfortunate percentage of teenage "Tarzan Christians" who come away from their spiritual "highs" beating their chests and swinging through the treetops, but who too often end up lost, demoralized, and defeated down on the jungle floor.

Surely at the heart of this oversimplification is the tendency of the church in general, and youth ministry in particular, to nurture in our students what the late pastoral theologian and counselor David Seamands referred to as a "childish faith."[13]

It's a jungle out there. We chop a path for our children around some of life's hardest questions during their younger years, and rightly so. But there comes a point at which the questions and dangers of the adolescent jungle are too many and too thick. All of a sudden our teenagers discover that the flannelgraph didn't tell the whole story. Doubt is a predictable part of adolescence. Some of our students make it through this thick undergrowth of questions with their faith intact and strengthened. Others end up losing the trail.

It's this part of the adolescent safari that we might think of when reading those familiar words of the apostle Paul: "When I was a child, I talked like a child, I thought like a child, I reasoned like a child. When I became a man, I put the ways of childhood behind me" (1 Corinthians 13:11). What Paul seems to be saying is that spiritual maturity involves giving up a *childish* faith that believes in easy answers, while still holding tight to a *childlike* faith that trusts the Father even when there doesn't seem to be any answer. Helping kids put away childish reasoning means nothing less and nothing more than helping them forge a path through the jungle, a path marked not by simple, easy half-truths, but by durable, biblical hard-truths.

That doesn't mean we should ever attempt to explain away the wonder and mystery of God. What it *does* mean is that we help the students in our youth group come to grips with the fact that life doesn't always look like the flannelgraph.

Notice in the chart on the next page the differences between "childish faith" and "childlike faith."

Childish Faith	Childlike Faith
• "Good Christians don't have pain and disappointments."	• God uses our pain and disappointment to make us better Christians.
• "God helps those who help themselves."	• God can only begin to help those who admit their own helplessness.
• "God always answers prayer."	• Sometimes God answers with "No" or "Wait."
• "Faith will help us always understand what God is doing."	• Faith will help us stand under God's sovereignty even when we don't have a clue what God is doing.
• "The closer we get to God, the more perfect we become."	• The closer we get to God, the more aware we become of our own sinfulness.
• "Mature Christians don't struggle with the tough questions of struggle and doubt."	• Mature Christians can wrestle honestly with tough questions because we trust that God has the answers.
• "Good Christians are always strong."	• Our strength is found in admitting our weakness.

Perhaps if we were to nurture in our young people something more than a childish faith, they'd find that faith to be more relevant when they're no longer children. Tarzan Christianity happens when we root students in a nice, clean, childish, flannelgraph faith instead of the childlike trusting faith to which Scripture calls us (Matthew 19:13-14).

Durable faith is always bred in the context of honest struggle with tough questions. So why do we sometimes find ourselves protecting our students from such questions? Because, as one writer describes it, growing young faith is like throwing rocks in a pond.[14] We know that hard questions and difficult conversations can break the stillness and serenity of unquestioned belief, and we realize that can cause waves that rock the boat of teenage faith. Or perhaps we've unconsciously bought into the false promise: "Blessed are those who make no waves, for they shall not suddenly find themselves in way over their heads in deep places."

Most of us have learned, sometimes through costly experience, that the ripples and waves of uncomfortable questions can move us to new places, places of deeper faith and closer intimacy with God. We rob our students of the joy of these faith discoveries when we try to keep them in the flat water of shallow belief. Tarzan Christianity is what happens when we shrink the faith down to flannelgraph questions, bumper-sticker-sized answers, and media-shaped simplicity. If we want to build in students a faith that lasts, we must move them from a faith that is childish to a faith that is childlike.

Imbalance 3: Too Much Feel Good, Not Enough Think Well

Neil Postman's excellent book called *Amusing Ourselves to Death* was published back in the mid-80s. Now, nearly three decades later, the provocative statement he makes to open the book sounds almost prophetic. In drawing a distinction between two popular notions about what the future might be, he comments:

> What Orwell feared were those who would ban books. What Huxley feared was that there would be no reason to ban a book, for there would be no one who wanted to read one. Orwell feared those who would deprive us of information. Huxley feared those who would give us so much that we would be reduced to passivity and egoism. Orwell feared that the truth would be concealed from us. Huxley feared the truth would be drowned in a sea of irrelevance. Orwell feared we would become a captive culture. Huxley feared we would become a trivial culture, preoccupied with some equivalent of the feelies, the orgy porgy, and the centrifugal bumblepuppy. As Huxley remarked in *Brave New World Revisited*, the civil libertarians and rationalists who are ever on the alert to oppose tyranny "failed to take into account man's almost infinite appetite for distractions." In *1984*, Huxley added, people are controlled by inflicting pain. In *Brave New World*, they are controlled by inflicting pleasure. In short, Orwell feared that what we hate will ruin us. Huxley feared that what we love will ruin us. This book is about the possibility that Huxley, not Orwell, was right.[15]

The current climate in youth ministry only confirms Postman's alarm. The church in general, and youth ministry in particular, has demonstrated more of an appetite for goose bumps than for God's truth, more interest in how our young people *feel* than how they *think*, more enchantment with the latest *Nooma* video than the latest book.[16] In short, we've become all heart and no head.

A personal experience comes to mind: Not long ago a youth leader approached me just prior to the last session of a weeklong camp. It had been a wonderful camp, and she said she knew the perfect way to finish out the week. "I have this song on my iPod called 'Thank You, Lord.' Why don't we play it for the kids in this last session?"

I was a little unclear about why she was suggesting this to me, since I had zero authority to make any decisions. So I encouraged her to talk to the folks in charge of the event.

And that's when she said, "Okay, I'll do that. But I think it would be really great. Every time I've played it at other camps, *everybody* cried..."

It was a totally sincere comment from a big-hearted leader who loves her students and wanted to maximize their experience during that week of camp. But the premise that lay behind her suggestion troubled me: If we can find a way to get all the kids crying, it must be a good programming idea. In other words, one of her criteria for evaluating a youth ministry idea was very simple: Does it make kids cry? Does it move them emotionally? If it does, it must be worthy.

Perhaps in this technological age we've come to desire the "human touch" so much that we now believe that any experience can be validated by its emotional impact—by its ability to "move" us. It's understandable that youth workers would think this way. Their constituents—the young people—have been taught to evaluate every experience by a simple question: Was it "good" or was it "boring"?

Perhaps another contributing factor is the overflow of educational theorists who seem embarrassed by the transfer of information—learning experts who've encouraged us to move away from teaching children facts, and identified the central task of the classroom as making all the students feel good about themselves.[17] This attitude is reflected in the words of James Ferguson, a former principal of

Heritage High School in Littleton, Colorado, who said: "It is more important for me to have students know how to read a map than for them to have any one bit of information about that map. Rather than knowing where Nepal is, it's more important that they know how to find Nepal." (In an earlier quote, Ferguson had actually opined that students needn't be able to find Florida. He later made the change to "Nepal," presumably because Nepal seems so much more remote and therefore manifestly not as important.)[18]

The thrust of Ferguson's comment seems quite clear: *It's not important for students to learn specific facts.*

In his book *Dumbing Down Our Kids: Why American Children Feel Good About Themselves But Can't Read, Write, or Add*, author Charles Sykes goes on to report of Ferguson:

> He specifically denied that high school students needed to be able to define either the Holocaust or World War II. When pressed, the educational leader would not even agree that a high school graduate should know something about the Great Depression. In one interview he implied that there was something unfair about singling out some historical landmarks as more important than others, a selection that was arbitrary, judgmental, and impertinent....In other words, students can be taught something called "map reading skills" or "geographical thinking."[19]

It's an interesting idea, and one that's quite prominent in the way a lot of youth workers think about teaching Christian doctrine. Such thinking is reminiscent of C. S. Lewis's comment about a conversation he once had with an old crusty R.A.F. officer. The officer complained that he had little need for Lewis' discussions of theology and doctrine for he had *felt God's presence* [emphasis added]: out alone in the desert at night, he'd sensed this mysterious, tremendous presence. Lewis's reflections are insightful for today's youth workers:

> Now in a sense I quite agreed with that man. I think he had probably had a real experience of God in the desert. And when he turned from that experience to the Christian creeds, I think he really was turning from something real to something less real. In the same way, if a man has once looked at the Atlantic from the beach, and then goes and looks at a map of the Atlantic, he also will be

turning from something real to something less real: turning from real waves to a bit of colored paper. But here comes the point. The map is admittedly only colored paper, but there are two things you have to remember about it. In the first place, it is based on what hundreds and thousands of people have found by sailing the real Atlantic. In that way it has behind it masses of experience just as real as the one you could have from the beach; only, while yours would be a single isolated glimpse, the map fits all those different experiences together. In the second place, if you want to go anywhere, the map is absolutely necessary. As long as you are content with walks on the beach, your own glimpses are far more fun than looking at a map. But the map is going to be more use than walks on the beach if you want to get to America.[20]

In short, our affection for creating emotional experiences and giving our students "warm fuzzies," coupled with our reluctance to teach biblical theology, is sending students to sea without any map. Our young people have become incapable of theological thinking because they don't have any theology to think about. Their faith is all heart (what they've felt of that "mysterious, tremendous presence") and not much head. And, as Paul warns us, it is this combination that leaves us as "infants, tossed back and forth by the waves, and blown here and there by every wind of teaching" (Ephesians 4:14).

From the interviews conducted by the researchers for the National Study of Youth and Religion, sociologist Christian Smith noted that few American teenagers made reference to any kind of "historically central religious and theological ideas."[21] Even though "the vast majority of U.S. teenagers identify themselves as Christian" and identify themselves as regular practitioners of their religious faith,[22] they seem to be essentially illiterate when it comes to the basic concepts of the Christian faith. Interviewers literally counted the number of times various key theological terms were used. Particular words, and their frequency of use, are noted on the following page:[23]

47	personally sinning or being a sinner
13	obeying God or the church
12	religious repentance or repenting from wrongdoing
9	expressing love for God
8	righteousness, divine or human
7	resurrection or rising again of Jesus
6	giving glory to or glorifying God
6	salvation
5	resurrection of the dead on the Last Day
5	keeping Sabbath (of 18 Jewish interviews)
4	discipleship or being a religious disciple
4	God as Trinity
4	keeping Kosher (of 18 Jewish interviews)
3	the grace of God
3	the Bible as holy
3	honoring God in life
3	loving one's neighbor
3	observing high holy days (of 18 Jewish interviews)
2	God as holy or reflecting holiness
2	the justice of God
0	self-discipline
0	working for social justice
0	justification or being justified
0	sanctification or being sanctified

Smith noted that when the teenagers did refer to *grace* in their interviews, it was usually in the context of the television show *Will and Grace*, not a reflection on God's grace. (Does that also count as a reference to free *will?*) While doctrinal understanding, of course, cannot be fully measured by word-use studies, it seems fair to say that our understanding of the basic tenets of Christian faith will be impaired if we don't have the language to talk about it. And American teenagers don't seem to have much of a vocabulary when talking about their faith.

Indeed, the NSYR research showed that among teenagers there is a widespread belief in what Smith called "Moralistic Therapeutic Deism" (MTD), a kind of vaguely religious Oprah-ism. It's *moralistic* because it conveys a vague sense of niceness; *therapeutic* because it's all about how it makes you feel; *and deism* because it points to a God who is impersonal, unattached, and generally uninvolved in the affairs of humans. The basic tenets of MTD, based on interviews with teenagers, are as follows:

1. A God exists who created and orders the world and watches over human life on earth.
2. God wants people to be good, nice, and fair to each other, as taught in the Bible and by most world religions.
3. The central goal of life is to be happy and to feel good about oneself.
4. God does not need to be particularly involved in one's life except when God is needed to resolve a problem.
5. Good people go to heaven when they die.[24]

Here's my summary of Moralistic Therapeutic Deism: *Barney goes to the Holy Land.*

Let me be clear: As a youth worker, I've seen the value of imaginative worship settings, cool videos, amazing media, powerful retreat experiences, passionate singing, and awesome mission projects. And I'm certainly aware that just spouting out doctrinal teachings in a classroom setting doesn't make them either memorable or worth remembering.[25] But where are Christian teenagers learning basic tenets of the Christian faith? And if they don't understand those basic truths or doctrines, as they've been articulated and embraced by our brothers and sisters in Christ over 2,000 years, then how does that impact their long-term faith?

I'm concerned that too much of our teaching is reduced to what can fit in a dark room and be communicated by a worship band illuminated by stage lighting and well-placed candles. Some may read this as a cheap shot at those elements of ministry. It certainly isn't meant to be. It's simply a way of saying that real-life discipleship involves *both heart and head.* Clearly, experience is an important part of the faith journey. Psalm 34:8 reads, "Taste and see that the LORD is good," not "Read Calvin's *Institutes* and see that the LORD is good." But that reality needs to be counterbalanced by Paul's reminder that "Faith comes from hearing the message" (Romans 10:17).

A youth ministry that moves students beyond Tarzan Christianity will offer a balanced programming diet of experience *and teaching* (Matthew 22:29). As Jesus put it in John 4:24, "God is spirit, and his worshipers must worship in the Spirit *and in truth*" [emphasis added].

Imbalance 4: Too Much "How To," Not Enough "How Come?"

Perhaps most troubling about the current state of youth ministry in North America is its infatuation with technique. Youth workers are far more concerned about *how* than *what or why*—technique is what captures the imagination, not *what* should we be doing or *why* are we doing it.

But *how* without *why* is empty and bankrupt. It's this same approach that assumes reading more books about *how* to have sex will breed deeper intimacy and greater sexual satisfaction. Any talk about love or commitment is understood as tedious and beside the point. Unfortunately, it's precisely this sort of thinking that's led to a culture in which marriages disintegrate with alarming frequency and sexual dissatisfaction seems far more the norm.

Of course, like everything else in Western culture, youth ministry in North America is market-driven. You don't have to play this game long to realize we've got to meet our students where they are—and good, innovative technique can help us do that better. But we want to be careful that the demands of the marketplace don't override the mandates of our calling as youth workers. Teachers with great communication skills can do more harm than good if they aren't teaching the right information. Doctors who have a remarkable bedside manner and know all the latest injection techniques won't do much good if they don't bring the proper cure. Holistic healing requires an understanding of both *how* and *why*.

We all understand that youth ministry presents us with some pretty tough how-to questions. And how-to books are especially helpful when we already feel time-stressed and under-trained. Even full-time, paid, veteran youth workers can appreciate the value of having an arsenal of resources that speak to the how-to issues. As a youth worker, I've personally benefited from many of these products through the years. Heck, I've *written* a lot of these books! So there's no doubt in my mind that it's worthy and appropriate to develop, publish, and provide training in the area of technique. If I'm a builder and someone develops a better hammer that will help me drive nails more securely or a saw that helps me cut more sharply, then I want that tool. Tools and techniques are good.

But far more important than the newest tool or technique is an understanding of what we're called to build. Hopefully, our commitment goes deeper than simply chaperoning, policing, organizing, feeding, programming, trip-planning, meeting-leading, and fornication-prevention. We do what we do to the glory of God— beyond what the youth group "market" demands of us, what our students or their parents expect of us, or what our congregations intend for us. Our commitment is to God. To move beyond Tarzan Christianity, we need youth ministry books, training, and resources that ask not just *how*, but also *what* and *why*. Otherwise, we'll waste time constructing higher, bigger tree houses and neglect our calling to build disciples.

IT'S A JUNGLE OUT THERE

These observations are incomplete. They deserve further attention and thought. But unless we address some of these concerns, we'll continue to see Tarzan Christians emerge from our youth programs. And it won't be for lack of screaming and swinging and swaying in the treetops; it will be because we haven't focused on the one absolute key: helping students learn how to cling to the Vine as they journey through the thick jungle of real life.

Thanks for reading this book. Please believe me when I say that, in my mind, your commitment to Jesus and to ministry with teenagers is heroic. I pray that my words here will help you think more clearly about that ministry and about how, by God's grace, you can turn hope into a reality. We move beyond Tarzan Christianity when we begin to focus our efforts on building a youth ministry that builds disciples. I hope this small book will help you gain a better grasp of that big idea.

NOTES

1. According to Barna researchers, "teenagers are consistently among the most religiously active Americans, with nearly six out of every 10 teens engaged in some type of group spiritual activity in a typical week" (*"How Teenagers' Faith Practices Are Changing,"* The Barna Group, posted July 12, 2010, http.barna.org/topics/teens-nextgen). As just one example of this apparent momentum, consider "See You at the Pole." Involving more than 3 million teenagers nationally and internationally, this annual event centers around teenagers who gather at flagpoles on their respective school campuses each September to pray for their teachers, administrators, and peers. From its humble beginnings back in 1990 at a youth discipleship retreat weekend in Texas, to a massive movement that involves a growing number of teenagers just two decades later, SYTP has many of the earmarks of an impressive work of God.

2. This book assumes that most of us recognize that youth ministry can look very different—depending, of course, on where in the world one looks. The general concerns raised by this book focus on youth ministry as it's commonly practiced in a huge portion of Western culture. Having traveled extensively overseas, I am constantly amazed at how youth workers in New Zealand and Australia struggle with many of the same issues as do youth workers in South Africa or Denmark or South Carolina or Vancouver. No doubt, the global homogenization of adolescence has a lot to do with it. Surely, much of it has to do with the pervasive and wide-ranging effects of Western culture. Part of it probably stems from the fact that most of us read some of the same youth ministry resources. But suffice it to say, the concerns in this chapter are generalizations. There are many churches and parachurch ministries doing substantial and significant youth work—and, admittedly, the observations here are anecdotal and personal in nature. They are more suggestive than conclusive. The questions raised in this chapter are offered not so much to end the discussion as to start it.

3. "Most Twentysomethings Put Christianity on the Shelf Following Spiritually Active Teen Years," The Barna Group, posted September 11, 2006, http://www.barna.org/teens-next-gen-articles.

4. Ibid. David Kinnaman, the principal overseer of the research, comments, "There is considerable debate about whether the disengagement of twentysomethings is a lifestage issue—that is, a predictable element in the progression of people's development as they go through various family, occupational and chronological stages—or whether it is unique to this generation. While there is some truth to both explanations, this debate misses the point, which is that the current state of ministry to twentysomethings is woefully inadequate to address the spiritual needs of millions of young adults."

5. Drew Dyck, "The Leavers: Young Doubters Exit the Church," Christianity Today, November 2010, 40, http://www.christianitytoday.com/ct/2010/november/27.40.html.

6. Ibid., 42.

7. My friend Rick Lawrence, editor of Group magazine, calls warnings like these almost "apocalyptic" in tone, and I sympathize with his concerns. He cites findings like those of a 2002 Gallup survey that suggest a much lower number of about 20 percent of churched young people stop attending church regularly as they move into their twenties. There are several possible reasons for the discrepancies between the various studies: the definition of "churched youth," the faith commitment of the youth surveyed (some studies survey Protestant youth, some Mormon youth, some Jewish youth, and some lump them all together), and the calculation used to determine church involvement of the young adults. (If a 22-year-old attends church once a month when she used to attend four times a month, has this young person disengaged or dropped out? And what if she pursues Christian fellowship from a source other than a local church?) For more discussion on these issues, see Tom Carpenter, "Busting the Drop Out Myth," Group, March/April, 2007, http://www.youthministry.com/?q=node/12450; Rick Lawrence, "A Bridge Over Troubled Water," Group, October 28, 2008, www.youthministry.com/bridge-over-troubled-water; and The Barna Group, "Most Twentysomethings Put Faith on the Shelf Following Spiritually Active Teen Years," posted September 11, 2006, http://www.barna.org/topics/teens-nextgen.

8. Dyck, "The Leavers," 42.

9. Ibid.

10. Just as an example, in one international survey of teenagers across eight countries as diverse as India, Thailand, Australia, Cameroon, the United States, and Great Britain, about one-third of youth surveyed said they talked at least once monthly about spiritual issues such as the meaning of life, faith, God, and why we're here on Earth. That means two-thirds of surveyed youth talk about spiritual

matters with their friends less than once a month. Of course, one could draw the conclusion that it's just not cool to talk about such matters in adolescent conversation. But it's also fair to suggest that if there were a wide-ranging awareness of spiritual hunger, it would be cooler to talk about it. Researchers go on to report that "the frequency of these conversations varied considerably across the participating countries. For example, only 19% of youth surveyed in Australia said they talk about the meaning of life with friends at least monthly, compared to 49% of youth in Cameroon. And 53% of Australian youth surveyed said they 'never' talk with friends about God or faith, compared to 10% of youth surveyed in Cameroon." When asked if they have conversations with friends about God or faith, 44 percent of the American teenagers said they happen at least once a month. But almost a quarter of that same group reported that those conversations "never happen." While nearly two-thirds of youth indicated that they'd spoken with their parents at least a few times in the past year about the parents' beliefs and faith, those conversations seemed pretty infrequent. "Only 24% indicate that they have these conversations at least once a month, and only 12% indicate that they have these conversations weekly" (Eugene C. Roehlkepartain, Peter L. Benson, Peter C. Scales, Lisa Kimball, and Pamela Ebstyne King, *With Their Own Voices: A Global Exploration of How Today's Young People Experience and Think About Spiritual Development*, The Search Institute, 2008, 16). All of this is to say, clearly, if youth workers want to reach a broad cross section of kids, there will be times when our conversation and programming will need to reach beyond "spiritual issues." Otherwise, we'll leave a lot of fish in the water.

11. See Christian Smith and Melissa Lundquist Denton, *Soul Searching: The Religious and Spiritual Lives of American Teenagers* (NY: Oxford University Press, 2005). The National Study of Youth and Religion surveyed more than 3,300 American teenagers from July 2002 to March 2003. It purports to be "the largest, most comprehensive and detailed study of American teenage religion and spirituality conducted" (p. 7) up to that time.

12. Kenda Creasy Dean, *Almost Christian: What the Faith of Our Teenagers Is Telling the American Church* (Oxford University Press: New York, 2010), 6.

13. David Seamands, *Putting Away Childish Things* (Wheaton, IL: Victor Books, 1983).

14. Kenda Creasy Dean and Ron Foster, *The Godbearing Life: The Art of Soul Tending for Youth Ministry* (Nashville, TN: Upper Room Books, 1998), 161.

15. Neil Postman, *Amusing Ourselves to Death* (New York: Viking Books, 1985).

16. In June of each year, the Creation Festival hosts the nation's largest Christian music festival in a beautiful mountain valley near Mt. Union, PA. It is a wonderful three-day event with over 50,000 in attendance in recent years. Each year, as a part of the festival, a rather large store sold books, music, and other merchandise.

But a few years ago, the managers of the store chose not to stock anything but music. When asked about this change in the merchandise, an assistant manager responded, "We couldn't get anybody to buy the books." The illustration is offered here not as an indictment of the Creation Festival as much as an warning to a church that won't listen to truth unless it's recorded in song or spoken in homily.

17. For a provocative study of this idea, see Charles Sykes' *Dumbing Down Our Kids: Why American Children Feel Good About Themselves But Can't Read, Write, or Add* (New York: St Martin's Press, 1995).

18. Ibid., 3.

19. Ibid. The late Richard John Neuhaus cites a relevant comment made by the Catholic novelist Walker Percy back in 1990, as he responded to yet another attack on the narrow-mindedness and dogma of the Roman Catholic Church. Percy wrote, "These issues could be debated, as indeed they often are, but here's how it appears to one novelist. If such attacks continue and are successful, the result will be pleasing mainly to the secular liberal establishment, who are in fact calling the shots, and destructive and divisive to the Catholic people. This novelist can only observe that if the magisterium and the sacramental orthodoxy of the Church are compromised in the name of 'creative pluralism' or suchlike, *there may be a lot of hugging and kissing and good feeling going on, but there won't be any Catholic novelists around. For these odd fellows are turned on precisely by these claims of the Church, breathtaking in their singularity and exclusivity, i.e., the magisterium and the Eucharist, and how these have endured with the people of God through these kinds of thicks and thins for two thousand years* [emphasis mine]. And they will endure despite these chic brush-offs of 'Rome.' Get rid of 'Rome' and what will be left in the end is California" (*First Things*, October 1999, p. 99).

20. Walter Hooper, ed., *The Business of Heaven* (New York: Harcourt, Brace and Co., 1984), 226.

21. Smith and Denton, *Soul Searching*, 167.

22. Ibid., 68.

23. Ibid., 167.

24. Ibid., 162.

25. For a great discussion on this, see Dean, *Almost Christian*, 144–184.

CHAPTER 2
AN INSIDE JOB

One of the great privileges of my life was a long friendship with the late Mike Yaconelli, the cofounder of Youth Specialties. Mike was a youth ministry pioneer, admired by many in the church as a slightly unorthodox latter-day prophet. Those of us who knew him well remember his easy laugh, his deep concern for youth workers, and his passionate walk with Jesus. His books touched countless lives with an invitation to what he called "dangerous wonder." When he gave me a copy of his book *Messy Spirituality*, he'd written inside the front cover these words: "Here's to growing old together." It was less than four days later that he died in a tragic single-vehicle accident in Northern California.

Of the many Yaconelli-isms that still shape my ministry, my favorite was this statement: "Youth ministry is not about you and teenagers; youth ministry is about you and Jesus. Teenagers are impacted by the overflow of that intimate relationship with Christ." It was a good way of affirming that the heart and soul of youth work begins in the hearts and souls of youth workers. Over and over, Scripture reminds us that God speaks *to* before he speaks *through*. Listening almost always comes before proclaiming.

> [v. 1] "The word of the LORD that came to Hosea… [v. 2] When the LORD began to speak through Hosea…" (Hosea 1:1-2).

> "He appointed twelve—designating them apostles—that they might be *with him* and that he might send them out to preach…" (Mark 3:14) [emphasis added].

Oswald Chambers observes:

So many are devoted to causes and so few devoted to Jesus Christ....
If I am devoted to the cause of humanity only, I will soon be
exhausted and come to the place where my love will falter; but if
I can love Jesus personally and passionately, I can serve humanity
though men treat me as a doormat. The secret of a disciple's life is
devotion to Jesus Christ...[1]

What it all means is that developing a ministry that builds long-
term disciples begins with building up the builders. It's a building
project that begins with the interior spaces of our lives. So before
we talk blueprints and tools, let's talk about what it means to be the
Carpenter's apprentice.

MOVING BEYOND THE STEREOTYPES

I was about two weeks into my first full-time youth ministry position when this sweet lady walked up to me after a Sunday morning
service and handed me the following document entitled "Church
Staff Job Descriptions." I've made a few edits to it so it's a little less
dated.

CHURCH STAFF JOB DESCRIPTIONS
Pastor:
• Able to leap tall buildings in a single bound;
• more powerful than a locomotive;
• faster than a speeding bullet;
• walks on water;
• gives policies to God.

Executive Pastor:
• Able to leap short buildings in a single bound;
• as powerful as a subway train;
• just as fast as a speeding bullet;
• walks on water if the sea is calm;
• talks with God.

Associate Pastor:
- Leaps short buildings with a running start;
- occasionally rides the subway;
- faster than a speeding BB;
- walks on water if he or she knows where the stumps are;
- talks with God before and after most board meetings concerning the budget.

Worship Leader:
- Can hurdle a keyboard (during contemporary service only);
- got started playing to passersby in a subway station;
- can fire a speeding bullet;
- swims well;
- is occasionally addressed by God—almost never through music written before 2001.

Youth Director:
- Runs into small buildings;
- eats at Subway on a regular basis;
- used a squirt gun in college;
- is an expert in water balloon warfare;
- lists God as a friend on Facebook.

Church Secretary:
- Lifts buildings to walk under them;
- kicks subway trains off the track;
- catches speeding bullets in her teeth;
- freezes water with a speeding glance;
- when God speaks she says, "May I ask who's calling?"

Part of what makes us smile at something like this is that it plays to stereotypes: the omnipotent senior pastor, the obnoxiously hip worship leader, the hapless youth pastor, and the scary church secretary. And, let's be honest, some of these stereotypes are true. (I won't say which ones!) But it's intriguing to consider some of the stereotypes that emerge when we think about people in ministry—particularly youth workers.

Some of us envision "Mike Macho," the ruggedly handsome, robust, all-around athletic stud who seems to win kids by the sheer strength of his natural abilities. He's the guy who beats the students to the top of the mountain on the backpacking trip. He plays guitar like Chris Carrabba. He has a shaved head and a carefully cultivated soul patch. He can bench-press the entire middle school group. And sometimes, just for fun, he catches Frisbees in his teeth as he glides by on his skateboard. And my own observation is that these people never have names like "Duffy"; it's always something like "Buck Studd" or "Rocky Montana"!

Of course, the stereotype of the perfect female youth worker is quite different. Let's call her "Joanna Joyful." She's always "so bubbly" and "so lively"; she "just loves those kids." OMG! She's on Facebook, like, 24/7 posting to her students. She always wears "neat" clothes and is "always in a good mood." She's, like, "totally amazing"...and, actually, it just sort of makes you want to vomit.

As you're reading this book, if the recurring thought swirling around in your brain is: "I must be crazy to think I can do this! I'm not the kind of person who can work with teenagers. I'm not even sure I can do ministry at all," then you need to know that you're not alone. Some of the greatest saints in the history of the church have been more than a little reluctant about responding to God's call. When informed by a church elder that the congregation had seen fit to call him apart for ministry, Martin Luther "advanced more than fifteen arguments" against the idea, and then promptly said, in essence, "Thanks, but no thanks." When the envoy continued to insist, Luther finally protested, "You are taking my life; I shall not live a quarter-year." To which the emissary replied, "In God's Name! Our Lord God has many things to do; He is in need of wise people in heaven, too."[2]

If there's one thing I've learned in youth ministry over the last 35 years, it's that there is no set personality type or temperament profile that describes an effective youth worker. I think of Bob, a youth pastor in Texas. He's been in youth ministry long enough to have been youth pastor to all of his own children, and he's still pouring his creativity and energy into new generations of teenagers. Or there's Jane, a married mother of three (including two teenagers) who's developed a wonderful ministry as a youth volunteer with her group in Atlanta. And Chris's behind-the-scenes style has been quietly nurturing teenage disciples and adult leaders in the same church in Indiana for more than a decade.

They are young. They are old. They are outgoing. They are quiet. They are everything from sports car to Jeep, Abercrombie to Wal-Mart, Starbucks to Buck's Barbecue, Conan O'Brien to Conan the Barbarian, Michael Scott to Mr. Rogers. There simply is no perfect résumé for youth work. Frederick Buechner notes our surprise at the folly of God "to choose for his holy work in the world…lamebrains and misfits and nitpickers and holier-than-thous and stuffed shirts and odd ducks and egomaniacs and milquetoasts."[3] Clearly, God isn't looking for "cool" people; God is looking for "called" people.[4]

But while the youth ministry stereotypes almost always get it wrong, there *are* some common qualities we see among youth workers who have staying power, youth workers—paid or volunteer—who are effective over the long haul. Building in students a faith that lasts will present its own kinds of unique challenges and opportunities. For a person whose heart is sensitive to those opportunities and whose imagination is suited to those challenges, the qualities that count are more inward in nature. Let's focus on four of them.

Quality 1: Diligence

> "And the one with the two talents also came forward, saying, 'Master, you handed over to me two talents; see, I have made two more talents.'"
>
> "His master said to him, 'Well done, good and trustworthy slave; you have been trustworthy in a few things, I will put you in charge of many things; enter into the joy of your master.'" (Matthew 25:22-23, NRSV)

There is perhaps no quality more important in a youth worker than diligence—being faithful to invest whatever gifts God has given us to maximize our impact for him. We all know youth workers who seem to have an infinite number of talents, everything from the gift of "guitar-ness" to the gift of "funniness" to the gift of "cool appearance and facial hair." But Scripture and experience bear testimony to the fact that the number of talents is not nearly as important as our willingness to make diligent use of the talents we've been given.

When the master of Jesus' parable confronted the unfaithful slave in Matthew 25 (verse 26), it wasn't because he had only one talent or because he lacked any particular ability. The master condemned him as a "wicked and lazy slave." Perhaps this servant was not as gifted as the others, but he should have made better use of whatever talent he had. He lacked diligence.

Most youth ministers learn early on that we can be either incredibly energetic and creative in our jobs, or woefully laidback and sloppy. And for the most part, very few people (oftentimes, not even the students!) will notice the difference. It's remarkable how few youth workers enjoy serious, constructive accountability. Nobody seems to know (or care?) what we're doing until something drastic happens (e.g., a bus breaks down, the kitchen is left a mess, porn photos are downloaded in the church secretary's office, someone made a call to the "Nasty Talk" 900-line on the church phone). So a youth worker who lacks the diligence to be a self-starter may well be a youth worker whose finish comes quickly.

There are two common mistakes we make in youth ministry— both of which are obstacles to true diligence.

The first is that we become self-obsessed, messianic, hard-driven people who seem to have forgotten that even God rested on the seventh day. Diligence is not the same as feverish activity. As one youth ministry vet put it, "The Father bids us to do his business, not to fill our schedules with busy-ness." We're not talking here about either legalism or clock-watching.[5] We're talking about earnest, responsible effort—making the best possible use of any and all talents we've been given by God.

For the volunteer, diligence might be manifest in the simple desire to take the ministry seriously—to approach it with creativity, excellence, conscientious effort, and genuine pastoral concern. It's a refusal to default into the habit of thinking, "Well, we could probably do more, but it'll be okay for teenagers...." For the professional youth worker, diligence may be something as simple as keeping regular office hours. To be sure, our work with teenagers will mandate a schedule that stretches beyond "9 to 5." On the other hand, church secretaries and parents are often frustrated by our aloofness and unpredictability. I recently called a youth worker only to be told by his secretary, "We have no idea where he is; we never do. You might try Taco Bell." It took an hour for my ear to thaw out.

The key is not activity, but productivity. In his excellent book *The Normal Christian Worker*, Watchman Nee puts it this way:

> It is not feverish activity of people whose restless dispositions keep them ever on the go that will meet the need, but the alertness of a diligent servant who has cultivated the upward gaze and can always see the Father's work that is waiting for his cooperation.... Jesus did not just come to make contracts with men; He came to seek them out and to save them....Some Christian workers seem almost devoid of any sense of responsibility; they do not realize the vastness of the field; they do not feel the urge to reach the uttermost ends of the earth with the Gospel; they just do their little bit and hope for the best.[6]

The second common obstacle to diligence in youth ministry is intimidation—the feeling that we simply aren't cool enough, talented enough, or young enough to impact a student's life for Christ. In the words of the unfaithful servant (Matthew 25:25), "I was afraid, and I went and hid your talent in the ground." And yet, a key element of this parable is that while each servant had a varying number of talents, *Jesus didn't mention any servant who had no talent.* Nor did he in any sense belittle the servant who had only one talent when the other servants were better endowed. The issue was never how many talents the servants had; the issue was whether each one invested his or her talents wisely.

I've seen many volunteer and professional youth workers through the years who either dropped out or burned out because they were constantly comparing their talents and abilities with the talents and abilities of other youth workers—focusing more on what they could *not* do than on what they *could* do. God is not limited by our self-evaluations of gifts, personality, or aptitude. (See Exodus 3–4; Jeremiah 1:6-8.) John Calvin described himself as "somewhat unpolished and bashful, which led [him] always to love the shade and retirement." And though he confessed to preferring to work in "some secluded corner where [he] might be withdrawn from the public view," God put him in a place of very public ministry.[7]

I believe very few people are simply *unable* to do youth ministry. The tasks of youth work are so diverse and the kinds of students so widely varied that I'm convinced most people can be effective with students if they're plugged into the right role and with the right amount of support. For one thing, youth ministry allows us to use lots of wonderful talents that aren't recognized elsewhere: the ability to hang out and get close to students; the ability to tell stories; the ability to make people laugh; the ability to ask good questions; and the ability to make biblical truth come alive through spoken word, graffiti, rap, drama, photography, dance, experiential worship, comedy, or just quiet conversation! In youth ministry, there's a place for almost every talent. (See 1 Corinthians 1:26-29.)

God is a Redeemer by nature; he does not waste any facet of a person's life and experience. That means God can use both our strengths and our weaknesses, our victories and our defeats, our trophies and our scars. When God called Moses, he made it very vivid: one man's snake on the ground is another man's rod in the hand (Exodus 4:2-4). God can take our mistakes and mishaps and use them as the staff by which we lead trapped people out of the bondage of sin and into the promise of God. What may appear to us to be the jagged shards of bad decisions and deep regrets can become—in the hands of God—centerpieces of his vocational mosaic. Such is the wonder of God's providence.

> "I knew nothing; I was nothing," one saint said about herself. "For this reason God picked me out." The world does not have many geniuses, but it can have many saints, for the life of a saint is open to all, even geniuses. What is required for a genius to become a saint is the same thing that is required of everyone, yielding to God. What matters is what God does with the capacities that people give over to God's use.[8]

The diligent servant accepts the fact that God has uniquely and adequately gifted each of us for the ministry to which he has called us (1 Thessalonians 5:14, 24). Our response is faithful obedience and investment.

Quality 2: Stability

> Therefore, my dear brothers and sisters, stand firm. Let nothing move you. Always give yourselves fully to the work of the Lord, because you know that your labor in the Lord is not in vain. (1 Corinthians 15:58)

I like to think of stability as nothing more than "stay-ability"—the ability to stay the course, the ability to stay with a work over the long haul, the ability to stay put when the going gets tough. It's a critical quality for those of us in youth ministry. It's the difference between a youth worker who blasts out of the gates for a quick sprint and the one who works with kids over the long run.

Youth work is not a ministry for the faint of heart. It's difficult. It takes us out of our comfort zones and leaves us feeling like we've landed somewhere just south of the Twilight Zone. We seldom get clear affirmation or clear direction in our work. Quite often our ministries are marked more by sowing than by reaping. As one youth worker put it, "God has allowed me to be part of some wonderful success stories. Unfortunately, my involvement was usually in the opening chapters before the story really turned good!" I like the way Mark Yaconelli put it: "If you have a group of twelve kids who don't understand your illustrations and one of them wants to kill you, you have a youth group just like Jesus."[9]

And yet, something about youth ministry seems to attract people who are more oriented to "feelings." These are people who at the end of the movie are more apt to say, "Oh my gosh, that was such a romantic movie!" than "Yeah, but in real life there's no such thing as vampires. And besides, sucking blood is so unsanitary." Maybe it's that ability to empathize and feel that makes us effective with kids. But it can also make us fickle, susceptible to discouragement and self-doubt, and subject to vast mood swings that hinge not so much on the unshakable promises of God as on whether or not last night's youth meeting bombed. Unfortunately, that kind of instability leads us to make bad decisions, snap judgments, and short-term choices. Watchman Nee has noted that the biblical account of Peter gives us a classic glimpse into instability fleshed out:

Peter's trouble was not just superficial. There was a fundamental flaw in his character. He was governed by his emotions, and his conduct was always unpredictable, as is the conduct of people who are controlled by their feelings. The enthusiasm of such people carries them at times to the loftiest heights; at other times depression drives them into the depths. It is possible for such people to receive divine revelation, but it is also possible for them to put hindrances in the way of the divine purpose....Brothers and sisters, it is woefully possible that our fancied love for the Lord is little more than sentimental attachment. Our emotional reactions to his love are not necessarily so deep or so pure as we think. We feel we love him utterly, but we live so much in the feeling realm that we think we are the kind of people we feel we are. We feel we want to live for him alone and want to die for him if he so wills; but if the Lord does not shatter our self-confidence as he shattered Peter's, we shall go on being deceived by our feelings and life will be one of endless fluctuations....The measure of our ability to follow the Lord is not assessed by the measure of our desire to follow him.[10]

The apostle Paul's example is very clear: "I have fought the good fight, I have finished the race, I have kept the faith" (2 Timothy 4:7). Consistency trumps charisma. Little wonder then that some of the final words he offers to Timothy are words of perseverance and stability: "But you, keep your head in all situations, endure hardship, do the work of an evangelist, discharge all the duties of your ministry" (2 Timothy 4:5).

Looking back over that short verse, what words jump out? *Keep, endure, hardship, work, duties.* These are words that get left off the bulletin announcements and recruitment letters. But they are now, and always have been, the terms that characterize faithful, fruitful, lasting ministry. We can sum it up with one word: *stability.*

And in case we're tempted to get stuck on that word, to imagine that youth ministry is all pain and no gain, well, Paul wants to be very clear about that as well. In the very next verse of this same passage he writes: "Now there is in store for me the crown of righteousness, which the Lord, the righteous Judge, will award to me on that day—and not only to me, but also to all who have longed for his appearing" (2 Timothy 4:8).

Quality 3: Vision

Very early in my ministry, I remember hearing these words: "A task without a vision is nothing but drudgery; a vision without a task is nothing but dreaming; but a vision with a task is a missionary." It's a truth that touches the very heart of effective youth ministry. I'm often asked what major principle I'd convey to someone just starting out in youth ministry, and I find myself consistently pushing for a vision: "What are you trying to accomplish? What would you like to see these students become? What is your vision?" The difference between youth-work-as-chaperone (keeping the order) and youth-work-as-shepherd (keeping the sheep) is vision.[11]

Vision is absolutely essential if we want to stay fresh and enthusiastic about youth ministry over the long haul. It's the chief prevention for burnout. I suspect that most of the time what we hear described as "burnout"—when someone runs out of steam—is more likely "blur-out"—when someone is without a clear vision in ministry and simply doesn't have anything to get "steamed up" about!

Dave began his work in inner-city Chicago with unusual optimism and expectancy. He dared to believe that God could raise up some new growth out of the burned-out stumps of urban blight. His vision was contagious. First, he got students excited, then their parents, and then other people around the neighborhood.

Before long, Dave was offered a chance to reclaim and renovate an old abandoned neighborhood movie theater. The place didn't look like much. It reeked from the garbage of neglect, vandals, drug users, and homeless people seeking shelter. What most people saw as a time capsule of dust, garbage, and destruction, Dave saw as a potential drop-in center and ministry headquarters.

Over the course of several months, Dave mobilized those kids and that neighborhood to make that vision a reality. Together, folks in one Chicago neighborhood transformed an abandoned building into a movie theater/youth activity center. It happened because one youth minister dared to dream big dreams for God. That's vision.

But vision is more than seeing what God can do with mortar and drywall. Effective youth ministries are stoked by men and women who have a vision for what God can do with real flesh and blood— the kind of youth worker who can hear a kid in the back of the van burping the alphabet, yet still believe this same kid may one day be a missionary on a distant continent sharing his faith in an equally amazing way.

It's not naiveté or fluffy optimism. It's the kind of Christ-centered realism that can look at the dust and decay of an abandoned student and trust in God's transforming power—the same power that took the Peter of the Gospels (brash, impulsive, inconsistent, and timid about his faith) and molded him into the Peter of Acts (faithful, bold, and outspoken). It is realism rooted first, in a biblical appraisal of who God is, and second, in a fair-minded recollection of what God has done in *our own* lives through the years. Without this vision for what God can do in the lives of our students, we'll be kicking Peters off the student leadership team because of one night's denial (John 18:15-27), or sending home a John Mark because of one instance of timidity (Acts 13:13; 15:36-39).

My friend Jack has that kind of vision. As a youth pastor, he was willing to take some risks with a college intern named Derek. At first, it didn't look like a very promising wager. Derek's attitude wasn't that great. He had a knack for saying the wrong thing at the wrong time, and he cultivated a sloppy personal appearance that made it hard for people to see beyond the externals.

As one of Derek's college professors, I have to admit I wasn't very hopeful. When Jack accepted Derek on his ministry team, my response was along the lines of, "Well, if you're really sure." I fully expected the arrangement to last no more than a few months. And, to be honest, there were several times when even that projection seemed optimistic. Jack would occasionally call my office, exasperated, and share another "Derek story."

And yet, the amazing thing is that every time Derek was corrected, he would respond. No matter how often he was taken down by rebuke, he always came back for more. Slowly but surely, miraculously and painstakingly, Derek began to change. Jack discovered that Derek had a remarkable gift of service. He could be given a task and, no matter how small it was, he'd get it done. Plus, the guy turned out to be a computer genius. He reprogrammed and debugged every computer in the church. He also began to show an ability to draw close to students.

In time Derek became a valued member of Jack's ministry team, well respected and appreciated. His story is a story of vision—the story of how one youth worker dared to take a chance on a student, looking beyond the negatives to see the positives that only he and God could see.

Before the ministry of speaking, before the ministry of touch (relationships), before the ministry of listening, there must be the ministry of *seeing*: Seeing beyond what *is* to what *could be*. The writer of Hebrews puts it this way: "Now faith is confidence in what we hope for and assurance about what we do not see" (11:1).

That's vision.

Quality 4: Integrity

It was the sort of interview so common now that we barely bother to read them anymore. Yet another Christian leader had fallen. It was obvious the interviewer was uncomfortable asking this renowned and respected pastor these questions. And yet, he pressed on with painful probing:

> INTERVIEWER: You have said there is no excuse for what you have done. In addition, you have insisted that sin be called sin. What factors contributed to the adultery?
>
> CHRISTIAN LEADER: It was a number of things....I was desperately weary in spirit and in body. I was working harder and enjoying it less.
>
> Satan's ability to distort the heart and the mind is beyond belief. I assume the responsibility for what I did; I made those decisions out of a distorted heart.
>
> In addition, I now realize I was lacking in mutual accountability through personal relationships. We need friendships where one man regularly looks another man in the eye and asks hard questions about our moral life, our lust, our ambitions, our ego.[12]

Integrity comes from the root word *integrate*, the ability to take various parts and knit them together into a unified whole. It is vital for youth ministry leadership because, through the course of our week, we walk into and out of a number of situations, each of which brings its own set of expectations, obligations, and responsibilities.

The average youth worker is trying to balance commitments to his or her spouse, children, friends, other family, family ministry, personal relationship with God, and (perhaps) a full-time job other than youth work. The list goes on and on. Integrating each of these commitments into a unified whole is the constant challenge of people in ministry. It's not easy. And in order to give what appears to be adequate attention to one area, it often means we're forced to neglect another area.

I remember watching an episode of *Captain Kangaroo* in which a guy kept about 30 plates spinning on top of sticks simultaneously. With music blaring he raced around the studio, jumping from one wobbling plate to another; and every now and then he'd suffer the loss of neglected chinaware that stopped spinning and crashed to the floor. I've seen youth ministers whose lifestyles suggest this same harried and hurried juggling act. No wonder we become weary "in spirit and in body" and find ourselves "working harder and enjoying it less." Integrity means weaving all that we are and all that we do into a consistent pattern of living.[13]

For youth workers, integrity begins with an absolute bedrock commitment to maintain intimacy with God. The greatest danger in youth ministry is that we become so enamored with the calling that we begin to neglect the Caller. We are so immersed in doing Christian work that we tend to mistake "doing" with "being and growing." Oswald Chambers warns us:

> Beware of any work for God which enables you to avoid concentration on Him. A great many Christian workers worship their work. Jesus told the disciples not to rejoice in successful service, and yet this seems to be the one thing in which most of us do rejoice. One life wholly devoted to God is of more value to God than one hundred lives simply awakened by His Spirit....So often we mar God's designed influence through us by our self-conscious effort to be consistent and useful. Jesus says there is only one way to develop spiritually, and that is by concentration on God.[14]

This habit of cultivating intimacy with God is what Eugene Peterson calls "working the angles."[15] He notes that there are three tasks or angles that shape any sort of ministry, whether paid or volunteer. As with the proverbial three-legged stool, the absence of any of these tasks leaves us unbalanced. The three tasks are—

1. **Prayer:** Focusing on what God is doing in one's own life;
2. **Scripture Reading:** Focusing on how God has worked in the lives of his people over the centuries;
3. **Spiritual Direction** (discipling, mentoring): Focusing on what God is doing in the life of another person.

It is no coincidence that each of these angles has at its heart a focus on God. This is always the central task of ministry—listening to God.

Unfortunately, there are three characteristics of this central focus on listening to God that tend to be foreign to most youth workers. First, it requires quiet, and youth workers tend to be a loud bunch. As a professional group, youth workers seem collectively to suffer from Attention Deficit Disorder. We are doers and movers, and listening to God requires stillness and quiet.

Second, none of these three acts—prayer, Scripture reading, and spiritual direction—is best practiced in public (at the front of the room). They require not just silence, but solitude—another element in short supply among most youth ministers.

Third, because none of these acts is public, it's easy to cheat. No one knows whether we're doing in private what we talk about in public. In fact, that's what makes the risk so acute. Most of our students assume we are so spiritual and so "in touch with God" that they give us the benefit of all doubt. And if we are not very, very careful, we will accept their appraisal of us as true, even when we know it is not.

It's a little ironic: Our very first priority as youth workers is to claim new ground in our individual relationships with God. And yet, that's the area of our lives that people actually know the least about. It's private, and to some extent, solitary; which is, of course, the reason we can so easily neglect it without being found out. As long as the ministry is moving along and we don't tip our hand, we could be dry as a bone spiritually without anyone knowing it. It is woefully easy in youth ministry to find ourselves doing what I call "third-person reading"—reading through a devotional not for what God might say to *us*, but for what God might say through us to *our students*. We begin to discover that more and more of our Bible reading is in preparation for a talk or a study, rather than for our own devotional refreshment.

Before we ever crack open that youth ministry resource book or read one more page of "how to have an incredible youth ministry," we need to stand face to face with the fact that we can't do this work on our own power (John 15:5). We lack not just the ability, but the grace, the patience, the love, and the hope that youth ministry requires of us.

Youth ministry veteran Barry St. Clair once told a story about a highway department worker who was busily painting lines down the middle of the highway. When his foreman inspected the work, he was unhappy to find that the lines were getting progressively fainter every few yards, until finally they could hardly be seen at all. When the foreman confronted the worker with his concern, the worker replied, "I can't help it. I'm trying, but I keep getting farther and farther away from the bucket."

You probably don't need another book that talks about how to get paint from the bucket. For those who are hungry, the bookstore cupboards are far from bare. But you may need a reminder that if you hope to paint solid lines of ministry that go the distance, then you'd better develop the discipline of bringing the bucket with you. God must be the first priority of your schedule. Integrity begins with a commitment to stay close to the Source.

GOT DISCOURAGEMENT?

Now, if you've just finished reading that last paragraph and you're now staring at this page blankly—but with the overwhelming sense that you're unstable, fickle, a slacker, a spiritual virus, and a danger to teenagers everywhere—cheer up! C. S. Lewis makes the point that, "When a man is getting better he understands more and more clearly the evil that is still left in him. When a man is getting worse he understand his own badness less and less."[16]

When I get dressed early in the morning, I may not realize that my shirt clashes with my sweater and my pants make my tie look weird. But by the time I get to my university classroom—once the sun is up, the lights are on, and students are offering to pray for my color blindness—the fashion sin is all too obvious. It was there all the time, of course, but it was exposed only by the greater light. The closer we are to the blazing light of Christ's holiness, the more we'll be aware that we fall pitifully short of his righteous standard.[17] Even a man as godly as John Wesley, when giving instructions about the epitaph for his tombstone, ordered that if there be any epitaph at all, it must include these words: "Here lieth the body of John Wesley, a brand plucked out of the burning...God be merciful to me, an unprofitable servant!"[18]

Youth ministry leadership has never been about perfection; it's about pursuit. (See Philippians 3:12-15.) Sure, God gives us in his Word some guidelines for those in leadership, and they're to be taken seriously.[19] But God has been using unworthy, ill-tempered, flawed, and minimally gifted people ever since the beginning of time. If we'll just submit ourselves to his Lordship and his healing grace, he can do the same with you and me.

NOTES

1. Oswald Chambers, *My Utmost for His Highest* (Uhrichsville, OH: Barbour and Co., 1935), 171.

2. Martin Luther, *Table Talk*, WA-T 3, #3143b; WLS 3, p. 1131, cited in Thomas C. Oden, *Pastoral Theology: Essentials of Ministry* (New York: HarperCollins, 1983), 26.

3. Frederick Buechner, *A Room Called Remember: Uncollected Pieces* (New York: Harper One, 1992), 142.

4. In fact, one of the advantages of the *introverted* personality is that it doesn't *need* people the way the extroverted personality does. Sometimes people go into ministry not because they have a love for people, but because they have a love for the *experience* of people. And while a love for the experience of people can be beneficial in ministry ("I just get energized by pizza, contact work, and sharing cabins and bathrooms on retreats..."), it isn't essential. Love for people is.

One is a love that is played out in quiet conversations—sometimes painful, sometimes difficult. The other is a love that is played out front and center—at the front of the room, in the center of attention. There are obvious pitfalls for the youth worker who loves only the experience of people. As one writer put it, "Our basic personality is a starting point, not a jail" (Charles J. Keating, *Who We Are Is How We Pray: Matching Personality and Spirituality* [Mystic, CT: Twenty-Third Publications, 1987], 118).

5. General William Booth, founder of the Salvation Army, once received the following letter from his wife: "Your Tuesday's notes arrived safe, and I was rejoiced to hear of the continued prosperity of the work, though sorry you were so worn out; I fear the effect of all this excitement and exertion upon on your health, and though I would not hinder your usefulness, I would caution you against an injudicious prodigality of your strength." [Author's translation: Don't be stupid about wasting your energy—even for causes that are *anything but* stupid.] "Remember a long life of steady, consistent, holy labor will produce twice as much fruit as one shortened and destroyed by spasmodic and extravagant exertions; be careful and sparing of your strength when and where exertion is unnecessary." (Cited in Gordon MacDonald, *Ordering Your Private World* [Nashville, TN: Thomas Nelson, 2007], 96.)

6. Watchman Nee, *The Normal Christian Worker* (Fort Washington, PA: Christian Literature Crusade, 1971).

7. John Calvin, *Commentary on Psalms, Volume 1.* http://www.ccel.org/ccel/calvin/calcom08.

8. E. Glenn Hinson, *Spiritual Preparation for Christian Leadership (Nashville,* TN: Upper Room Books, 1999), 182.

9. Cited in Mark DeVries, *Sustainable Youth Ministry: Why Most Youth Ministry Doesn't Last and What Your Church Can Do About It* (Downers Grove, IL: InterVarsity Press, 2008), 39.

10. Nee, *The Normal Christian Worker,* 30.

11. The intent of this book is to suggest just the sort of vision that could shape and animate a youth ministry. But for more detailed information about forging a personal vision for your own ministry, see Duffy Robbins, *Youth Ministry Nuts and Bolts (Revised and Updated): Organizing, Leading and Managing Your Youth Ministry* (Grand Rapids, MI: Zondervan, 2010), chapter 5.

12. *Christianity Today,* "A Talk with the MacDonalds," July 10, 1987.

13. For practical help on personal management, see Duffy Robbins, *Youth Ministry Nuts and Bolts (Revised and Updated): Organizing, Leading and Managing Your Youth Ministry* (Grand Rapids, MI: Zondervan, 2010), chapter 4.

14. Chambers, *My Utmost for His Highest*, 116.

15. Eugene Peterson, *Working the Angles* (Grand Rapids, MI: Eerdmans, 1987), 2–5.

16. C. S. Lewis, *Mere Christianity* (New York: Macmillan Publishers, 1952), 93.

17. Note Paul's own confession in 1 Timothy 1:15-16. This awareness of one's own sin can be quite healthy, to a point. The Puritan preacher of colonial times, Thomas Goodwin, observes, "When I was threatening to become cold in my ministry, and when I felt the Sabbath morning coming, and my heart not filled with amazement at the grace of God, or when I was making ready to dispense the Lord's Supper, do you know what I used to do? I used to take a turn up and down among the sins of my past life, and I always came down with a broken and contrite heart, ready to preach, as it was preached in the beginning, the forgiveness of sins....Many a Sabbath morning, when my soul had been cold and dry for the lack of prayer during the week, a turn up and down in my past life before I went into the pulpit always broke my heart, and made me close with the gospel for my own soul before I began to preach." (Cited in Gordon MacDonald, *Facing Turbulent Times* [Wheaton, IL: Tyndale, 1981], 93).

18. *The Journal of John Wesley*, Percy L. Parker, ed. (Chicago: Moody Press, 1974), 198.

19. See 1 Timothy 3:1-13; Titus 1:6-9.

CHAPTER 3
IT'S ALL ABOUT RELATIONSHIPS

Several years ago, a Korean artist named Gwang Hyuk Rhee completed a remarkable piece of art depicting the figure of Jesus standing with outstretched arms. Surrounding Jesus on this six-by-four foot scroll are 27 angels symbolizing the 27 books of the New Testament. Even if it had been a traditional painting, it would be an amazing work of art.

But, upon closer observation, what makes this piece of work even more incredible is that the artist created this image not through sketch work, drawing, or brushstrokes, but by writing out the entire New Testament with a fine point pen, shading various letters and words so the images of Jesus and the angels would appear on the scroll. In other words, the figure of Jesus is actually created by the words of the New Testament text. It took the artist two years to write out the entire 185,000-plus words of the New Testament, shading each letter in just such a way that the detailed portrayal of Jesus and the angels would be clearly visible on the scroll. He did it because he wanted to capture vividly this one idea: *The Word became flesh.*

In his devotional book *The Word Became Flesh*, E. Stanley Jones observes that the artist, through his painstaking and meticulous work, is giving us a powerful testimony to the miracle of what we sometimes refer to as *incarnation*.[1] It's a word derived from the Latin word *carnis*, which means "flesh" or "body." It's akin to the word *carne* in Spanish, also translated as "meat." That's why we call it *chili con carne* because it's *chili with meat* (that is, unless you're in the school cafeteria, in which case it's *chili without carne*). From the original Greek of the New Testament, it's translated as "flesh."

In John 1:14, the incarnation is announced in stunning, straightforward terms: "The Word became flesh and made his dwelling among us." The declaration is stunning because John already told us in verse 1, "In the beginning was the Word, and the Word was with God, and the Word was God." So this is nothing less than a proclamation that God—the God who authored all of creation—came to this planet with meat on his bones: God became flesh. Like a playwright who steps onto the stage of his own play, or a painter who steps into the canvas of his own painting, the Creator chose to be a part of what he created. One writer described it as a shoemaker becoming a shoe!

That in itself is pretty stunning, but John goes on to affirm that not only did God become a human being, but *God lived among us*. In fact, it's kind of fascinating to watch different translators wrestle with how to capture the wonder of these words:

- "The Word became a human being and...*lived among us*" (Good News Translation).
- "So the Word became human and *made his home among us*" (New Living Translation).
- "The Word became flesh and *made his dwelling among us*" (New International Version).
- "And the Word...became flesh...and *tabernacled (fixed His tent of flesh, lived awhile) among us*" (The Amplified Bible).
- "The Word became flesh and blood, and *moved into the neighborhood*" (The Message).

Clearly, the big idea is that God came down and came very close. In fact, if you've been camping or backpacking with someone, the Amplified Bible's image of God "fixing His tent among us" gives a vivid picture of just how close God has come! Little wonder, then, that we celebrate Jesus as *Immanuel*, which means "God with us."

MINISTRY BECOME FLESH

Why is this so important? Because somewhere between the sketches of that old drawing and the words of this familiar passage is a truth that bring us right to the heart of a ministry that builds teenagers into lasting disciples of Jesus. The central mandate of youth ministry is to be incarnational—to flesh out the Word of God to the students with whom we are working, to consistently, creatively, and obediently live out the Word of God in their presence. We can't talk about building disciples without talking about building relationships. It's being willing to do ministry in that place where theology meets geography. Paul put it this way:

> In your relationships with one another, have the same mindset
> as Christ Jesus:
> Who, being in very nature God,
> did not consider equality with God something to be used to his
> own advantage;
> rather, he made himself nothing
> by taking the very nature of a servant,
> being made in human likeness.
> And being found in appearance as a man,
> he humbled himself
> by becoming obedient to death—
> even death on a cross!
> (Philippians 2:5-8)

The way of Christ's ministry points us beyond the safe walls of a youth room plastered with Christian posters, and challenges us to be *among* kids—on their turf, on their terms. Sad to say, too many of us adopt more of a "Little Bo Peep" approach: "Leave them alone and they'll come home, wagging their tails behind them." We've stayed back at the church and waited for the lost sheep to flock to our meetings. It's an approach that leaves lots of kids ravaged by the wolves of ever-present temptation, false promises, empty hopes, and broken hearts. And, as we saw in chapter 1, even those who seem to have joined the flock may—once they've moved into middle and late adolescence—wander off, get lost, and end up chasing after a hundred different pseudo-shepherds.

INCARNATION: A MINISTRY OF BEING THERE

For me, one of the scariest parts of fatherhood was teaching my older daughter, Erin, how to operate a motor vehicle. Teaching her to drive our manual transmission car was an exercise in faith. She's an extremely bright young woman, but she never seemed to grasp the delicate dialogue that takes place between clutch and accelerator—that when one speaks, the other must be quiet. Consequently, whenever the car lurched into forward motion, we were jolted by a sequence of quick, punishing whiplashes: dashboard... headrest...dashboard...headrest. I can still remember how she'd occasionally look over at me with her beautiful eyes wide open and say, "Daddy, how come when I'm driving, you can't control your saliva?" And I'd have to explain, "Sweetheart, Daddy's being whip-lashed into oblivion."

Day after day, week after week, these driving lessons were tough! It was intense. There was anger. There were tears. There was yelling. There was pouting. And then, of course, she'd also get emotional.

But no matter what happened during the lesson, when we got back to the house, it was always the same thing: We'd walk in the front door, my wife would meet us there, and she'd look into my eyes and say, "Don't forget why you're doing this...*don't* forget *why* you are doing this..."

She was reminding me of something we all know intuitively: *There are certain truths we simply cannot communicate from a distance.* My daughter was not going to fully comprehend the principles of safe driving by reading the *Pennsylvania Driver's Manual.* She wasn't going to fully embrace those truths simply because she heard them in a driver's education classroom. She wasn't going to be impacted by those ideas just because she watched some scary movies about defensive driving. The only way she was going to really learn those truths was if I got out there in the car with her, on the road with her—in good times, bad times, uphill, downhill. I needed to be there *beside her.* That's the only way it works because some truths simply cannot be communicated from a distance. That's a little something of what we mean by *in-car*-nation!

Clearly, God understood that if we were ever going to comprehend his love for us, it would have to be done in a way that was up close and personal. It couldn't just be the Word became words. It would have to be the Word became flesh, God incarnate. Jesus said, *"Come to me…"* (Matthew 11:28), not just *"listen to me."* One of the essential qualities of lasting youth ministry is that it's relational. We don't just read the operator's manual to kids, we join them on the journey—in good times, bad times, uphill, downhill.

Our students are much more likely to remember what we've said while we're walking beside them than while we're standing in front of them. Is it any wonder that in three years of public ministry, Jesus spent only a fraction of his time preaching to large crowds and the bulk of it in the company of individuals and small groups of disciples? Just as copper is a conductor of electricity, relationships are the conductors of lasting faith. One of my mentors drove this principle home to me with these words: "If you want to make a big impression, Duffy, speak to a crowd; but if you want to make a big impact, speak to a person."

"LOOK WHERE YOU ARE"

Years ago, I heard a story about Mary, a high school counselor who was discouraged because she couldn't seem to connect with one particularly notorious group of girls at her school. One day, out of deep frustration, she finally asked one of the girls what the problem was, why they never responded to her efforts to reach out to them. Without a pause, the girl blurted, "Well, just look where you are!" Mary was sitting behind her desk in an air-conditioned office, which was across the hall from the office of the dean of women—a place where these girls were sent for disciplinary reasons on a regular basis.

It was a simple comment, but it helped open Mary's eyes to see that part of the problem was geography. If she wanted to impact those girls, she was going to have to be *among them*, she needed to *move into their neighborhood*. So Mary did some research and discovered that this group liked to hang out around the cafeteria door that led to the parking lot. The location was hot and unpleasant, since it was near the school's boiler room, but it allowed them to smoke and skip classes.

That summer, after the school year ended, Mary got permission to move her office. And she found the perfect location, very close to where these girls hung out—inside the school's boiler room! She had to work through all sorts of red tape with her principal and the school board members (who all assured her it was very unprofessional to locate her office in that location). But she did it. And at the beginning of the next school year, she noticed a real thaw in her relationships with these girls. They realized she was serious about being their friend; they even nicknamed her "Moms."

Mary was still the same person she'd been before. All that had changed was her geography. But the change signaled to those girls that Mary would do whatever it took to have a relationship with them. Notice what that young woman said to her: "Look *where* you are." Not "You're too old," "You're not cool enough," "You don't know enough about our music," or "You don't have a three-color tattoo with the face of a pirate," but *"Look where you are."*

How many kids are unwilling to draw near to Jesus because those of us who love Jesus have been unwilling to draw near to them? You can almost hear Paul writing, "Though being in very nature an adult (counselor/administrator), she did not consider air-conditioning something to be used to her own advantage…but humbled herself— even to the level of the boiler room!" That's a good picture of incarnational youth ministry.

CLAIMING HOLY GROUND

If we hope to shape youth ministries that are incarnational, the first question we have to ask ourselves is, "Where are our students?" If we want to develop a ministry that goes where kids are and dwells among them, then we'd better do some serious thinking about where those kids are located.

Youth ministry veteran Dean Borgman refers to this question/ investigation process as "exegeting the community." It sounds complicated and difficult, but it's really just another way of saying we need to explore—to look carefully—at our respective communities. It might be as simple and as profound as driving around your community after school or on a Friday night just to see where the kids are spending their free time. Or it might mean taking the time to talk to kids in the neighborhood where your ministry is based. You could begin by talking to the teens in your church, or the kid who mows your lawn, or the kid who serves you a burger, or the kid who baby-sits your children.

Mary found out about the kids in her school by simply keeping her eyes and ears open. Students are usually the best source of information, but there are others: school counselors, parents, and even fellow youth workers. Sometimes the most effective firsthand research of the teenage world involves going to a football game, volunteering to chaperone at a school dance, serving as a tutor at school, or becoming a coach for a youth sports team. What we're really talking about here is what the apostle Paul described as "walking around and looking carefully" (Acts 17:23). I suspect Jesus would have described it as a good shepherd looking for lost sheep (Luke 15:4-7).

The crucial questions we want to ask are these:

1. Where are the students in our community? For some communities, the big Friday night sport is partying. In other communities, kids spend all their time at the beach. In still others, a majority of the teenagers spend their time sitting in front of a convenience store or hanging out at the mall. And for others, most of the action takes place at school sporting events. As you and your ministry team dream about a more incarnational ministry, begin by asking where the "boiler room" is in your community.

2. What are the various groupings among teenagers in our community? The average high school might have anything from jocks to nerds to skaters to zipperheads to dexters to gangstas to band freaks to druggies. It doesn't take many hours in the school cafeteria before it becomes apparent that each subgroup has its own closed society with its own set of standards and behaviors. The party animals are sitting in their corner of the cafeteria chugging milk cartons; the jocks are bench-pressing the tables in their section; the band freaks are over by the vending machines talking about clarinets; and then there are the head bangers who are sort of off in their own area, but they aren't saying anything because they can't hear one another!

You'll quickly discover that there is very little "cross-pollination" between these groups. Unlike the youth ministry of yesteryear, it's no longer a matter of reaching "key kids" whose popularity will win us an audience with less popular students. If we're really seri-ous about reaching as many students as possible, the key will be to develop relationships that penetrate each of these small friendship clusters—"pitching our tent among them." To do that effectively, we need to understand who these groups are—boiler room, band room, computer lab, and locker room.

Canadian researcher Donald Posterski began talking about these "friendship clusters" more than two decades ago:

> A friendship cluster is more than just a circle of relationships. It is a heart and soul of being young today. It is a place to belong. There is no formal membership. You are either in or you are not. Being in means you share many things: interests, experiences, intimate thoughts, problems, and triumphs of the day. Being in means you tune into the same music, wear each other's sweaters, and generally just enjoy each other.[2]

In more recent research, youth ministry veteran Chap Clark expands on our understanding of friendship clusters by describing them as a family of midadolescents (roughly 14 to 18 years old) who are bound together, almost like a tribe, around one "unifying social narrative"—*who we are* and *who we're not*. Understanding something about those clusters and respecting their importance in the adoles-cent world is critical.

3. What are some of the socioeconomic realities of our community? Is this environment rural, urban, or suburban? What kinds of families live in our area? How many of our students are from single-parent families? Blended families? What is the median income? What are the major kinds of employment? A lot of the hard data is probably available through a township office or from the local planning commission. But we can get a sense of the big picture by simply keeping our eyes and ears open and being sensitive to these kinds of issues.

4. What kinds of agencies are already at work in our com-munity? What are the needs we can meet? With which agencies might we be able to network to better serve the community without duplicating efforts? What other youth ministries are serving this area? It's a great relief when we understand that our youth program doesn't have to be some kind youth ministry Wal-Mart that offers every possible service under one roof. One way we can care for teenagers is by being aware of others in the community who also care for teenagers.

But much of what we've described so far can be done at a distance, and incarnational ministry is never really done from a distance. If we want our students to become life-long disciples, we begin by building lasting relationships with them. Kenda Creasy Dean explains:

> Youth *ministry* focuses on relationships, not only because of who teenagers are but because of who God is. God is a relationship—Christian tradition uses the relational language of Father, Son, and Holy Spirit to describe the persons of the Trinity—and this God's love is so generous the Godhead alone cannot contain it. Significant relationships with other Christians matter because they teach us something about what *God* is like—the One who can love us in spite of ourselves and who loves us passionately enough to suffer willingly on our behalf.[3]

DWELLING AMONG THEM

When I first began doing youth work, I was working as an intern with a parachurch mission whose primary vision and focus was to reach out to unchurched high school students. I spent many a lunch hour walking (and sometimes stalking) a campus, trying to develop relationships with students who not only didn't know me, but apparently didn't feel any great desire to know me. Honestly, at least at first, those were some of my most awkward experiences in youth ministry. I was constantly asking myself: *Will they wonder why I'm here on their campus? They know I'm not a student. They know I'm not a faculty or staff person. They know I'm not a parent. That leaves only a narcotics officer, a sex criminal, or an axe murderer!* It was a genuine cross-cultural outreach, and I wasn't at all sure how the natives of this culture were going to respond.

Perhaps you've felt some of this uneasiness as well. Leaving the safe places of adulthood to be among the loud, sometimes troubling, sometimes threatening places of adolescence is not a comfortable experience for most of us. This is probably why teenagers have suffered what Chap Clark calls "systemic abandonment," the largely unintentional—and sometimes absolutely intentional—cultural toxin that separates teenagers from adult relationships. Of course, we provide allowances, rides, youth rooms, programs, sports teams, and opportunities that "empower young people to make their own decisions." But too often what we don't provide is ourselves. As Chap puts it:

> We have evolved to the point where we believe driving is support, being active is love, and providing any and every opportunity is selfless nurture. We are a culture that has forgotten how to *be* together....Even with the best of intentions, the way we raise, train, and even parent our children today exhibits attitudes and behaviors that are simply subtle forms of parental abandonment.[4]

It's a reality that only adds to the challenge of being there for our students—faithfully, unconditionally—because it adds to our discomfort their suspicion and skepticism. They wonder if they're safe with us, if we can be trusted with their hurts and hopes. After all, they aren't exactly used to having adults seek them out for the purpose of friendship.

In the world of adolescence, it's understood that if an adult wants to talk with you, then more often than not it's usually a bad sign. Most of us remember from our own schooldays the forbidding "Ooooooohhh!" that followed the public address announcement that someone should "please report to the office." Such an invitation almost always spelled trouble. We all seemed to understand intuitively that this person wasn't being invited to the office because the principal was lonely. I was surprised to discover this same uneasiness even in my own daughters at home. I'd say, "Hey, Erin and Katie, can you guys come downstairs for a minute?" And, inevitably, their response would be, "Are we in trouble?"—as if the only time we allowed them on the ground floor of our home was for torture. "Yes, come on down. Your mom's got the machete. Be brave. This will build character."

But incarnational youth ministry calls us to move beyond our intimidations. And as I continued to spend time with students in my own ministry, one truth came back to me over and over again:

Kids are open to, and will find time for, genuine, sincere love. It won't be easy for most of us, but here are some practical guidelines to remember:

Incarnational witness will be more signpost than sales. There are two basic approaches to witness: One is signpost; the other is sales. The difference between the two is fundamental: signposts point the way; salespeople try to close the deal. Scripture offers us a pretty vivid picture of the signpost approach in the charge Moses gives to parents in Deuteronomy 6:

> Love the Lord your God with all your heart and with all your soul and with all your strength. These commandments that I give you today are to be on your hearts. Impress them on your children. Talk about them when you sit at home and when you walk along the road, when you lie down and when you get up. Tie them as symbols on your hands and bind them on your foreheads. (Deuteronomy 6:5-8)

What's pretty clear here is that incarnational witness goes beyond an institutional schedule. One of the basic principles of the signpost approach is that God often works better *between* lessons, *after* the club meeting is over, and *beyond* church property. A hallmark of Jesus' own ministry is that his style of witness wasn't some canned, rehearsed sales pitch. It was a consistent lifestyle of living out and talking about the kingdom of God.

It's intriguing to read the words of those disciples on the road to Emmaus: "Were not our hearts burning within us while he talked with us on the road and opened the Scriptures to us?" (Luke 24:32). Much of the time, Jesus' greatest work was done "on the road," in transit while he was walking with his disciples, boating with his disciples, ministering with his disciples, praying with his disciples, or eating with his disciples.

One of my most memorable "Emmaus discussions" with a group of students took place around a campfire one night along the Appalachian Trail after a delicious dinner of Spam, rice, and cream of mushroom soup. (Our hearts were "burning within us," too!) It seemed like the least likely place for heavy-duty spiritual conversation, but somehow we began talking about what it meant to be a Christian—and it was amazing. I heard questions and shared in discussions that night that I hadn't experienced in a year of Sunday school and youth meetings.

Why *then*? Why *that* night? We had no media, no praise band, none of the trappings that we consider so essential for relevant ministry today. We didn't even have enough light to read a Bible. There's no good reason for the way God showed up that night, except my group decided to go deeper at that particular time and place—and God chose to join us in the conversation.

Resist the temptation to be the "Answer Man." Even the most cursory study of Jesus' teaching in the Gospels will show that he taught more often by asking questions than by giving answers. It's noteworthy that on the road to Emmaus that day (Luke 24:13-33), Jesus never identified himself to the two disciples. It's true that he "explained to them what was said in all the Scriptures concerning himself" (24:27), but that was only after they'd thoroughly aired their own questions and doubts.

Our tendency as youth workers is to want to immediately correct any wrong statements about God, to make sure we point out areas of sin and error in a student's life. We shouldn't be surprised to learn that's a pretty quick way to close down communication. The average teenager is not that interested in playing "Ask Mr. Spiritual." That doesn't mean we must be silent about our faith or feelings. But it *does* mean that we may need to walk a while with our students and hear their questions before we start "explaining" everything.

One of the oldest principles of incarnational ministry is that we must "earn the right to be heard." As one preacher put it: "No one cares how much you know until they know how much you care." Sometimes the most powerful testimony comes from a mouth that is closed long enough to listen to a heart that is open.

Contact work is not about "acting like a teenager." The key to contact work is not acting like a teenager. Teenagers don't need more peers. They have plenty of peers. Nor do they need more parents. I've never heard a teenager comment, "Dude, my life would be so much better if I had, like, two or three more parents."

The incarnational youth worker is neither a peer nor a parent, but a priest—someone who will share like a peer and care like a parent (see 1 Thessalonians 2:7-12), but whose great desire is to bring a

student into a closer relationship with Jesus. One of the most important principles of incarnational ministry is simply this: Teenagers
don't need adults who act like teenagers. They need adults who won't
freak out when *teenagers* act like teenagers.

**You cannot build an in-depth relationship with every stu-
dent on every campus in your community.** Focus on building
relationships with a few students. No matter how much compassion
you have, it's impossible to hug a group of 30 people. They must
be embraced one at a time. So the genius of team ministry is that
it allows different people with different personalities and different
interests to build real friendships with individual students, instead
of one person trying to befriend a mob.

**Don't feel threatened because you're able to relate to some
students better than others.** It's completely normal that you'll
connect more easily with certain students. Students relate to some
of their peers better than others, too. A youth worker who is athletic
is obviously going to have an affinity with students who are more
athletic. And likewise, the leader who has musical ability will have
a natural rapport with students who are musical. Personally, I've
found I have an almost instant connection with kids who are expe-
riencing premature hair loss. It's a small niche, but it's *my* niche! So
don't feel weird about having a natural connection with a certain
group of students. Again, that's why a team of leaders can embrace
more students than an individual working alone.

A word of caution here: In every youth group I've ever been a
part of, there are always a few kids who seem to relate to nobody.
Chances are, even as you read those words you probably had at least
one name and face come to mind! We won't be in youth ministry
for long without learning the fine art of hugging porcupines. And as
much as we need to be freed from the notion that we are the messiah
for every student, we can't ever forget that every kid needs to know
the true Messiah. And when it comes to those difficult, sometimes
sullen, sometimes argumentative, sometimes cold and unresponsive
students, we need to pray for the Spirit of Jesus to enable us to reach
beyond our preferences and natural alliances and love those who
are hard to love. The incarnate God talked with people no one else
would speak with (John 4:7-9), touched lepers that no one else would

get close to (Matthew 8:1-4), and felt the pain that everyone else ignored (Matthew 9:20-22).

Trust me, I understand it's easier to write this in a book than live it out in faithful ministry. But some of the great stories of faith have started out with hard chapters of unbelief and open antagonism. And in so many of those stories, there was an obedient youth worker who overruled his or her natural inclination to keep a distance and drew closer in obedience to God's call. Next time you have one of those hard-to-reach students in your group, remember Ananias.

When the Lord asked Ananias to show hospitality to the freshly converted Paul, Ananias had every reason to be wary. After all, Paul had been arresting, persecuting, and killing believers *just like Ananias*. But what Ananias could not have known was that, through his acts of kindness and hospitality, Paul the persecutor was on his way to becoming Paul the apostle. And, fortunately, Ananias was willing to care beyond his comfort zone.

> "Lord," Ananias answered, "I have heard many reports about this man and all the harm he has done to your holy people in Jerusalem. And he has come here with authority from the chief priests to arrest all who call on your name."
>
> But the Lord said to Ananias, "Go!" (Acts 9:13-15)

We worry that we can't reach these students because we don't have the right words, don't know the right answers, or can't find the right means of approach. But incarnational ministry is about being *among* the students, spending time with them, and living life in such a way as to become a consistent signpost pointing to Jesus. Quite often, that happens not because someone has just the right words, or a snappy answer, or even the right gesture to thaw a cold encounter. If Mary's story reminds us that boiler rooms sometimes become sanctuaries, then Ananias's story reminds us that sometimes hostility melts in the face of godly hospitality.

Learn to love the sinner, even while hating the sin. Dick was a Young Life leader in the Southeast who had a knack for getting close to students. As we led club together, I was continually amazed at his ability to befriend kids whom everybody else deemed undesirable and unreachable.

It took me about a year to realize why I didn't seem to be enjoying the same success: It was as if I expected these students to act like Christians or else I wasn't going to share Christ with them. I wanted kids to come to our group, but I wanted them to come *on my terms*. I was so busy letting these kids know—both verbally and nonverbally—that I didn't approve of their lifestyles, they just naturally assumed that neither I nor my God would accept someone as sinful as they were. I had to learn how to love these kids without feeling like I was somehow condoning their behavior.

One of the most common barriers to incarnational ministry occurs when we can't get beyond a teenager's music, appearance, language, or behavior to see a hurting and lonely kid who needs to be shown the love of Jesus. We can't embrace someone we're unwilling to touch. And that means taking the first step of unconditional love and outreach.

When Jesus approached the Samaritan woman for a drink of water on that hot afternoon (John 4:1-26), she was disarmed and surprised. "How can you ask me for a drink?" the woman asked (4:9) because Jesus was a Jew and Jews didn't normally associate with Samaritans. If we're reaching out to the lepers and outcasts of the high school, then we'll probably be met with the same skepticism and suspicion. And yet, if we're willing to be flexible enough to accept students as they are, then we're likely to find an openness and a thirst that runs much deeper than their unattractive behaviors.

Every conversation doesn't have to be an in-depth proclamation of the gospel. The freedom of incarnational ministry is that we are *living out* the message, fleshing out the Word in the presence of students. That might mean spending an entire afternoon with a group of students without ever directly mentioning Jesus, sin, the Trinity, or four views on millennialism.

To be sure, there will be times for specific conversations about spiritual matters. But it is not a lost opportunity or a betrayal of calling to simply be present without making a gospel presentation. Talking with students about their lives, their concerns, their areas of interest—that may be the kind of vital ministry that prepares the ground for later sowing of the seed. Of his own incarnational style, Paul wrote, "Because we loved you so much, we were delighted to share with you not only the gospel of God but our lives as well" (1 Thessalonians 2:8).

That's not to say that sharing the gospel is unimportant. It's *very* important. A highway sign that simply says YOU ARE HERE… AND THIS SIGN IS HERE WITH YOU without offering any further direction or instruction is of very little help to the lost traveler. Understanding what we believe and why we believe it are fundamental elements of being a disciple-maker. But neither is it enough for the sign to be absolutely accurate and have all the needed information posted, but be planted in a location that's too high up for the traveler to see or too far away from the traveler's route.

Incarnational ministry is a ministry that joins shared life with shared faith. That's why we call it *Word become flesh*. Word without flesh is hollow and unconvincing; flesh without Word is a signpost with no instructions. There are those who like to cite St. Francis's dictum: "Preach the gospel always, and if necessary, use words." It's a great reminder of the importance of lived-out witness. And that's good. But as a ministry methodology, it falls short of the approach of Jesus who—although he was pretty doggone Christlike—*still felt compelled to use words.*

AN EMBRACE THAT SPEAKS LOUDER THAN WORDS

The book of Acts offers us a parable of incarnational ministry in an obscure episode we witness from Paul's own ministry:

> Seated in a window was a young man named Eutychus [Author's note: a typical student in the back of the room], who was sinking into a deep sleep as Paul talked on and on [Author's note: a typical youth worker]. When he was sound asleep, he fell to the ground from the third story and was picked up dead. Paul went down, threw himself on the young man and put his arms around him. "Don't be alarmed," he said. "He's alive!" Then he went upstairs again and broke bread and ate. After talking until daylight, he left. The people took the young man home alive and were greatly comforted. (Acts 20:9-12)

So often, discouragement in youth ministry comes through those students who sleep through the sermon, make inappropriate body noises during the Bible study, and giggle during the prayer time. The all-too-common youth worker response is to leave them "for dead."

This passage reminds us, though, that sometimes a warm hug is more powerful than a hot talk. Paul's preaching put Eutychus to sleep, but his embrace brought the young man back to life. That's a principle we must never lose sight of if we want to disciple teenagers. There's no question that sermons and Bible studies and talks are all important parts of the process of building disciples. But even the most effective preaching is still the Word become word. The triumph of the gospel of Christ is that it is the Word become flesh.

NOTES

1. E. Stanley Jones, *The Word Became Flesh* (New York: Abingdon, 1979).

2. Donald C. Posterski, *Friendship: A Window on Ministry to Youth* (Scarborough, Ont: Project Teen Canada, 1985), 8.

3. Kenda Creasy Dean and Ron Foster, *The Godbearing Life: The Art of Soul Tending for Youth Ministry* (Nashville, TN: Upper Room Books, 2005), 27.

4. Chap Clark, *Hurt: Inside the World of Today's Teenagers* (Grand Rapids, MI: Baker Academic, 2004), 46–47. Clark reflects: "There is simply too much cumulative weight that points to a disturbing trend: The way midadolescents have been forced to design their own world and separate social system has created perhaps the most serious and yet understudied social crisis of our time." (p. 43)

CHAPTER 4

A CLEARLY DEFINED VISION

Lorne Sanny, one-time president of the Navigators, once recounted that back during the Civil War there was a bit of confusion in the high command of the Union Army. It seems that President Lincoln couldn't dissuade his generals from launching an attack on Richmond, Virginia. Why the generals had this obsession with capturing Richmond is unclear, but they were bound and determined to make their assault. Growing in his exasperation, Lincoln challenged his strategists by asking why they were so set on attacking Richmond when, in fact, the Confederate Army was not *in* Richmond. Finally, the story goes that one day, in a fit of frustration, Lincoln blurted out, "Gentlemen, what good will it do us if you capture the city of Richmond? Even if you win in Richmond, all you will do is gain geography. Sirs, we're not out to gain geography; our purpose is to win a war!"[1]

I'm not sure the story is completely true (and when an illustration works well for me, I'm usually not inclined to investigate it any further). But I'd like to make two observations about Sanny's account.

Observation 1: I have to admit that in some ways I sympathize with those generals. I don't have a military background, and I'm certainly not a keen evaluator of military strategies. But honestly, if I were a general facing the jaws of heated combat, I might lean toward a battle plan that centers on attacking where the enemy *isn't*.

Observation 2: Our purpose in this short history lesson is to consider how easy it is—even in youth ministry—to spend our resources fighting the wrong battles and working toward the wrong objectives in grand efforts that don't really help us gain victory in the mission. We strategize and scheme about how we can win our own youth ministry "Richmonds"—bigger groups, more activities, better facilities—only to discover that gaining geography is not the same as winning the war. That's why it's so important for those of us in youth ministry to be absolutely clear about our mission, to be single-mindedly focused on why we do what we do. That will be our task in this chapter, and it's going to come down to four big ideas.

Building in students a faith that lasts means building:

- a ministry with a focus on Jesus;
- a ministry that calls students to service;
- a ministry that nurtures mature faith;
- a ministry that builds community.

We'll look at each of these mandates in some detail, but let's begin with the big picture.

"GO AND MAKE DISCIPLES..."

In one sense, it's really quite simple: As youth workers our mission is to make disciples. The mandate of Matthew 28:19-20 is as clear now as it was two millennia ago. Jesus' followers are commanded, "Therefore *go and make disciples* of all nations, baptizing them in the name of the Father and of the Son and of the Holy Spirit, and teaching them to obey everything I have commanded you" (emphasis added). Over the years the church has called this command "the Great Commission." Some have commented wryly that, in reality, it has become "the Great Omission"! Like much of the church, we youth workers seem to have forgotten that our number-one priority is not to build well-organized programs, or edgy ministries with the latest media razzle-dazzle, or busy youth groups that keep kids in the orbit of an active youth program. What we are called to do is "make disciples." Youth ministries that build programs without building disciples are doing little more than launching an attack on Richmond. It might gain us some geography, but it won't win the war.

"Ah, yes, but what is a disciple?"

Christians have a lot of different notions about discipleship. Some would say that a teenage disciple of Christ is a young person with short hair and middle-class values who doesn't "smoke, drink, cuss, chew, or go out with girls who do." Others might imagine a student who has consistent daily devotions, memorizes Scripture, fasts on a regular basis, and attends some weekly service of worship. Still others will think of a teen who's engaged in worthy causes and service projects designed to communicate hope and healing to a hurting world. And, of course, there are those who'd argue that a *real* disciple is all of the above.

In chapter 1 we affirmed a simple notion: God makes converts; we make disciples. But if we start with that premise, then what does it mean to be a disciple?

Before you read any further, take a moment to jot down your basic definition of a disciple of Jesus:

Somebody who is following Jesus and learning from Him. Not someone who seems to be perfect, but someone who is constantly growing and becoming more like Jesus every day.

Disciple was Christ's favorite word for those whose lives were linked with his. The Greek word for *disciple*, *mathetes*, is used 269 times in the Gospels and Acts. Essentially, it means "one who is taught" or "a trained one." But what is the nature of that training?

There are two sets of passages listed below. The first set includes three passages from the Gospel of John in which Jesus talks about discipleship. The second group comes from a single passage in the

Gospel of Luke in which Jesus makes three statements about discipleship, each time using a variation on the basic formula: "If a person...*[a different condition in each statement]*, then that person *cannot* be my disciple." Read through these passages to sharpen your own sense of what it means to be a disciple, and then write out your thoughts below. How do these passages refine or inform your definition of discipleship?

Set 1
John 8:31

John 13:34-35

John 15:1-8

Set 2
Luke 14:25-33 (especially verses 26, 27, and 33)

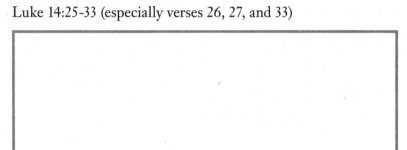

These verses offer just a sampling of Jesus' words about what it means to be his disciple. But even if we were to draw from all 269 New Testament verses in which we come across the word *disciple*, there is the danger that our picture of discipleship won't be as color-ful, or as vivid, or as broad and expansive as the one God gives us in Scripture. Trying to reduce *discipleship* to simple definition is a little like trying to understand *dance* without thinking about music and rhythm. Discipleship can never be reduced to simple steps.

The Greek word that's often translated as "disciple" is rooted in a word that means "to learn" (*manthano*). Clearly, back in the first century when the New Testament was written, the word was used to refer to adherents or followers of a great master—not just a teacher-student relationship, but a master-follower relationship.[2] Yet, there's confusion about what that master-follower relationship with Jesus might look like in the twenty-first century. Just think of the many different youth ministry entities that are described as "discipleship groups"—some are intentional about serious commitment, others are little more than social groups who meet occasionally and chat. Are they all really *discipleship* groups—and, if not, what makes a *dis-cipleship* group a *discipleship* group?

Part of this question is rooted in the distinction we made between "converts" and "disciples" in chapter 1. But is it really possible for a person to be truly converted in any kind of meaningful way with-out, in fact, becoming a disciple? How we answer that question will obviously have a very real impact on how we build a ministry that builds disciples. So let's look across the youth ministry landscape and consider some of the prominent ideas we find there about what it means to be a disciple:

- **Some suggest that a disciple is a serious seeker.** Because of the original meaning of the Greek root word, some contend that disciples of Jesus are students who are seeking to learn about Jesus. In this view, a teenage disciple might not be a convert (i.e., a Christian) at all, but someone honestly seeking to *learn* the way of Jesus. In fact, one writer takes this even a step further by saying: "That the terms 'disciple' and 'Christian' are not synonymous is clear from John's Gospel. 'From this time many of his disciples turned back and no longer followed him' (John 6:66). Then there was Judas, *an unsaved disciple.*"[3] (emphasis added)

- **Others believe a disciple is a committed follower of Christ**—sort of Christianity with an upgrade. Of course, a lot of people are troubled by the notion that a nonbeliever could be called a *"disciple."* We worry that such a view dulls the New Testament edge of discipleship that's implied in passages like Luke 14:25-33. They suggest that the word *disciple* should be reserved only for serious *Christians who've made a commitment to follow Jesus and obey his radical demands.*[4] In other words, while view number one supposes it's possible to be a non-Christian and be a true *disciple*, view number two suggests it's possible to experience Christian conversion and *not* be a *disciple*. In this view, some Christians simply haven't reached the point where they're willing to be radical for Jesus. They're believers; they're just not "on-fire" believers. They're converts, but not disciples. Listen to the words of one writer explaining this view: "There is a vast difference between being saved and being a disciple. Not all men who are saved are disciples although all who are disciples are saved."[5]

- **Still others believe that every true Christian is a disciple.** Those who hold this third view are concerned that discipleship is sometimes thought of as an optional second step in the Christian life, like an elective course for overachiever Christians who wish to go beyond conversion. They argue that such thinking cheapens what it means to be a Christian and cheapens the grace that allows us to be called by that name. In other words, the Christian who is not a *disciple* is not a Christian either. In this view, authentic conversion will always yield the fruit of authentic discipleship.

Dietrich Bonhoeffer, in his classic work *The Cost of Discipleship*, made precisely this point: "Cheap grace is grace without discipleship, grace without the cross, grace without Jesus Christ, living and incarnate....Happy are they who know that discipleship simply means the life which springs from grace, and that grace simply means discipleship. Happy are they who have become Christians in this sense of the word. For them the word of grace has proved a fount of mercy."[6]

This view sees *discipleship* as synonymous with the Christian life, a process that begins at conversion and continues in an ongoing process of growth. James Montgomery Boice explains it this way: "Discipleship is not a supposed second step in Christianity, as if one first becomes a believer in Jesus and then, if he chooses, a disciple. From the beginning, discipleship is involved in what it means to be a Christian."[7]

It's possible to defend each of these positions on biblical grounds. But listening to the whole melody and rhythm of Scripture, one observation is absolutely unavoidable: By the time of the book of Acts, *disciple* was the term used to describe those who were *true believers in Jesus*. And while there might be some wiggle room about what constitutes a "true believer," James makes it vividly clear in his epistle that true belief will always be manifest by works of love and obedience (2:14-24). Talking about a genuine conversion that isn't manifest in genuine discipleship is like talking about a genuine birth that isn't followed by genuine life.[8] It just doesn't make much sense.

AN APOSTLE'S PORTRAIT OF DISCIPLESHIP

One of the best ways to get a vivid, practical portrait of discipleship is to look at how it plays out in the New Testament church. After all, Paul's letters are the words of a guy who's seeking, with all of his energies, to build churches that build lasting disciples. In Ephesians 4:11-16, the apostle is writing to the church at Ephesus about how disciple-making will be incorporated into their common life. We're going to focus on this passage for two reasons: (1) Implicit in Paul's words is a vision for the church, the body of Christ; and biblical youth ministry is always going to be connected, either directly or indirectly, to growing the church; and (2) Paul's practical style of writing allows us to observe in very down-to-earth terms what disciple-making actually looks like.

Read through the passage slowly—twice—and then we'll look at it in more detail.

> [11] So Christ himself gave the apostles, the prophets, the evangelists, the pastors and teachers, [12] to equip his people for works of service, so that the body of Christ may be built up [13] until we all reach unity in the faith and in the knowledge of the Son of God and become mature, attaining to the whole measure of the fullness of Christ. [14] Then we will no longer be infants, tossed back and forth by the waves, and blown here and there by every wind of teaching and by the cunning and craftiness of people in their deceitful scheming. [15] Instead, speaking the truth in love, we will grow to become in every respect the mature body of him who is the head, that is, Christ. [16] From him the whole body, joined and held together by every supporting ligament, grows and builds itself up in love, as each part does its work. (Ephesians 4:11-16)

Reading through this manifesto for the church, the apostle Paul gives us four key elements that characterize a ministry which builds faithful disciples of Jesus.[9] Let's do an inventory of each of these four essential elements.

Essential 1: Focused on God in Christ

"We will grow to become in every respect the mature body of him who is the head, that is, Christ." (Ephesians 4:15b)

The number one goal of youth ministry is not tithing, church membership, voter registration, political mobilization, retreat attendance, recruiting students to invite their friends, denominational involvement, tattoo avoidance, sin management, or sales of T-shirts/light bulbs/ candy/spaghetti/cookies/Christmas cards/glow-in-the-dark posters of the pastor. It is helping students develop a love relationship with God. Our Lord said, "'Love the Lord your God with all your heart and with all your soul and with all your mind.' This is the first and greatest commandment" (Matthew 22:37-38).

Our mandate as youth workers—whether paid or volunteer, Sunday school teachers or small group leaders, in local churches or in parachurch settings (Young Life, Youth for Christ, Fellowship of Christian Athletes, Jedi for Jesus)—is to help students love God and develop a relationship of growing, deepening intimacy with God through his Son, Jesus. In a youth ministry culture where program direction is more common than spiritual direction, Eugene Peterson's earnest warning to pastors has a haunting relevance for youth pastors as well:

> We get asked to do a lot of things…most of which seem useful and important. The world of religion generates a huge market for meeting all the needs that didn't get met in the shopping mall. [Youth] pastors are conspicuous in this religious marketplace and are expected to come up with the products that give customer satisfaction. Since the needs seem legitimate enough, we easily slip into the routines of merchandising moral advice and religious comfort. Before long we find that we are program directors in a flourishing business. We spend our time figuring out ways to attractively display god-products. We become skilled at pleasing the customers. Before we realize what has happened, the mystery and love and majesty of God, to say nothing of the tender and delicate subtleties of souls, are obliterated by the noise and frenzy of the religious marketplace.

> But then who is there who will say the name *God* in such a way that the community can see him for who he is, our towering Lord and Savior, and not the packaged and priced version that meets our consumer needs? And who is there with the time to stand with men and women, adults and children in the places of confusion and blessing, darkness and light, hurt and healing long enough to discern the glory and salvation being worked out behind the scenes, under the surface. If we all get caught up in running the store, who will be the [youth] pastor?[10]

It's in the interest of maintaining this emphasis that Kenda Creasy Dean refers to youth workers as "Godbearers." It's a plea she makes based on these words from Luke 1:26-38—

The angel went to her and said, "Greetings, you who are highly favored! The Lord is with you."

Mary was greatly troubled at his words and wondered what kind of greeting this might be. But the angel said to her, "Do not be afraid, Mary; you have found favor with God....The Holy Spirit will come on you, and the power of the Most High will overshadow you. So the holy one to be born will be called the Son of God..."

"I am the Lord's servant," Mary answered. "May your word to me be fulfilled."

Reading these words of mystery and promise, we have to wonder how it might change our views of youth ministry if we actually thought of our service as youth workers in terms of Mary's awesome and wonderful privilege of bearing Christ for the students with whom we have contact. How might that change the way we think about that conversation at Starbucks, or that small group gathering, or that short devotional on Sunday night, or that all-nighter that seemed to last all week? Dean suggests that we sell ourselves short when we define our ministry solely in terms of the relational element—caring relationships, an encounter with a caring adult or caring community. The wonder of our work is that youth ministry isn't just relational; it's also *incarnational* (an encounter with God).[11]

One practical implication of all of this—even if it makes some of us a little uncomfortable—is the value of giving our students basic theological instruction. We sounded this theme in chapter 1, but it bears repeating here. Christian Smith, lead researcher in the National Study of Youth and Religion, comments:

> Our findings suggest to us that religious communities should also stop...presuming that U.S. teenagers are actively alienated by religion, are dropping out of their religious congregations in large numbers, cannot relate to adults in their congregations, and so need some radically new "postmodern" type of program or ministry. None of this seems to us to be particularly true....Most religious communities' central problem is not teen rebellion but teenagers' *benign "whateverism."*[12] (emphasis added)

Every now and then, when reminded of the need to teach theological truth to our students, I'll hear some earnest youth worker comment, "Look, I'd rather my students *know* God than just *know about* God." And it's a sentiment I fully understand. Of course intimacy with God is more important than cold, theological knowledge. But this line of thinking breaks down when it presents a false dichotomy (or distinction) between knowing God and knowing about God. The fact is, it simply isn't possible to know God without knowing something about God.

If someone is asked, "Do you know Duffy Robbins?" and answers yes, then the assumption is that this person knows certain facts *about* Duffy Robbins. For example: He is a Caucasian male who lives in Valley Forge, Pennsylvania; he teaches youth ministry at Eastern University; his hairstyle favors a large three-inch part; he has two daughters, a son-in-law, and two exceptional grandkids; he has the diet of a nine-year-old; he tweets at least once every two months or when the moon is aligned with Jupiter; and he speaks a lot to teenagers and people who love teenagers. Of course, someone could know all those things about Duffy Robbins and still *have no relationship with him at all.* And some who *do* know me personally might well agree that that would be preferable! But all of us would agree that *knowing* Duffy Robbins is much more than knowing those facts *about* Duffy Robbins.

To claim to know Duffy Robbins without knowing anything *about* him simply makes no sense. In the same way, we can't divorce the mandate of helping students know God from the necessity of helping students know *about* God. In other words, a youth group that offers warm, God-shaped fuzzies without helping students understand the basics of who it is we believe in and what we believe about him comes about as close to making disciples as watching an episode of *Oprah*. Although it will probably take some of us out of our comfort zones, building in students a faith that lasts means giving them some instruction about that faith.

Kenda Creasy Dean makes this point by asking some extremely penetrating questions:

> What if the blasé religiosity of most American teenagers is not the result of poor communication but the result of excellent

communication of a watered-down gospel so devoid of God's self-giving love in Jesus Christ, so immune to the sending love of the Holy Spirit that it might not be Christianity at all? What if the *church* models a way of life that asks, not passionate surrender but ho-hum assent? What if we are preaching moral affirmation, a feel-better faith, and a hands-off-God instead of the decisively involved, impossibly loving, radically sending God of Abraham and Mary, who desired us enough to enter creation in Jesus Christ and whose Spirit is active in the church and in the world today? If this is the case—if theological malpractice explains teenagers' half-hearted religious identities—then perhaps most young people practice Moralistic Therapeutic Deism not because they reject Christianity, but because this is the only "Christianity" they know.[13]

Another note of caution to be raised here relates to the fact that as youth workers we often do a better job of cultivating a commitment to youth group than a commitment to the Lord. Of course this is unintentional. It begins innocently enough by encouraging students to come to youth group. We remind them how much fun youth group is and how critical it is that they have weekly fellowship with their Christian friends. And we do that partly because we know it's true, and partly (a pretty big part) because we want them to come back to youth group next week! But over time, if we're not careful, there's a subtle trap that snares both us and our students: We end up nurturing their commitment to youth group more than we nurture their commitment to Jesus.

As a youth minister in Rhode Island, I once had the pleasure of having a student approach me and say with complete sincerity, "You know, I haven't been in youth group the last five weeks. And I've got to be honest—in that time my spiritual life has just gone right down the tubes!" Of course, on the outside I was all furrowed brow and full of concern. But deep down there was a part of me thinking, *You bet it has, kid. And don't you forget it. You'd better never miss a week with this youth group again!* I didn't realize it until later, but the subtext of my attitude was: "You'd better believe your spiritual life tubed out when you missed youth group for five weeks; because without this youth group, all you have is…God." (!) We tend to forget that within a few years, the kids we're working with now *won't* have the youth group. All they *will* have is God.

It's almost as if we've forgotten that our main purpose in youth ministry is to help students move forward on that pilgrimage of growth through which they become progressively more dependent on God and more intimate with God, while becoming progressively *less* dependent on the second-hand feeding that comes through youth group. If we're building students whose faith is dependent primarily on a weekly skit, a creative Bible study, or a summer camp that is "the best week of your life," then we're building Christians whose faith simply won't sustain them beyond the high school years.

Mark Yaconelli puts it well:

> All youth ministries engage youth in practices; however, not all practices within ministries with youth are beneficial or even Christian. For example, a youth ministry that engages youth solely in forms of entertainment may train youth to relate to God in passive observance. If discipleship only involves lectures on moral living, then youth may relate to God only through how well they are able to live moral lives. If youth ministry revolves around study and memorization, then God may only be known in the intellect. A youth ministry grounded in Christian practices will pay attention to the whole way of life promoted in the content and activities of the ministry. It will seek to offer youth tools and give them opportunities to practice life lived in imitation of Christ.

> How do we determine if a practice is Christian? …All Christian practices begin in *prayer*, invite personal *confession*, take place within the *worshiping community*, and bear fruit in *solidarity with the poor* in communion with the Spirit of Jesus Christ. It is our availability to love within these four relationships—God, ourselves, the faithful, and the poor—that is the hope of all faithful practices.[14]

Authentic discipleship always points our students back to Jesus. We begin with him, we end with him, and we journey with him at all points in between (Hebrews 12:1-3). Little wonder that Paul writes,

> So Christ himself gave the apostles, the prophets, the evangelists, the pastors and teachers, to equip his people for works of service, so that the body of Christ may be built up until we all reach unity

in the faith and in the knowledge of the Son of God and become mature, attaining to the whole measure of the fullness of Christ. (Ephesians 4:11-13)

Read through this verse again, find the word *until*, and circle it. It's key here because it's a destination word. It points us to where we're going as disciples and what we're building in youth ministry when we build disciples. And what it points to is a destination of being so focused on Christ that, over time, we become more and more like him (1 John 3:2-3). Paul writes that this is our destiny (root word = *destination*) as people created in the image of God (Romans 8:29). We do what we do *until*, or to the end that, our students are becoming like Jesus. Building in students a faith that lasts begins with the clear priority of helping students to know, embrace, and enjoy God through his Son, Jesus. Anything less is a strategic attack on the wrong objective.

Essential 2: Calling Students to Service

"To equip [God's] people for works of service." (Ephesians 4:12a)

When Jesus cited love for God as the essence of the first and greatest commandment (Matthew 22:37-38), he went on to connect it with a second commandment: "The second is like it: 'Love your neighbor as yourself.' All the Law and the Prophets hang on these two commandments" (22:39-40). Reflecting on these words, the great fifth-century patriarch Cyril of Alexandria commented: "Therefore the first commandment teaches every kind of godliness. For to love God with the whole heart is the cause of every good. The second commandment includes the righteous acts we do toward other people."[15]

The plain fact is that God has called all Christians to service.[16] All of us are called to do the work of ministry (Ephesians 2:8-10; Colossians 3:23-24; 1 Peter 2:9-10). That's as true for teenaged Christians as it is for older Christians. Any definition of spiritual growth that doesn't include some evolving understanding that God calls each of us to a life of ministry in some shape or fashion is a definition of spiritual growth that is foreign to the clear teaching of Scripture.

Unfortunately, our general unwillingness to call students to a commitment of ministry and service to neighbor—to accomplish something bigger than themselves—lives right down to the low expectations students generally have for themselves. We don't challenge them to attempt very much because we don't expect they'll be willing to accept the challenge. And our students are often reluctant to accept the challenge because they assume they'll be incapable.

I remember one ninth grade girl in our youth group who seemed so quiet and shy that I really couldn't see her in any kind of leadership role. Due in part to my own insecurity, I didn't dare trust her to lead a small group for our youth program. Her poor self-image and low profile in the youth group were very likely a reflection of my unwillingness to give her a shot at a leadership position. I just didn't think she had the stuff.

I finally worked up the nerve to let her give it a try. To my absolute surprise and bewilderment, she was incredible. Kids actually began requesting her as a small group leader. Her personality blossomed. The group discovered her, and she continued as a strong student leader throughout her high school years.

Of course, we all love to hear stories like that—and how much more do we love to *tell* stories like that? But they seem pretty mythical when you're standing in front of a group of sleepy-eyed, bored 15 year olds who seem more interested in when someone will serve the Cheetos than how they can serve Christ. It's hard to imagine that Jesus could ever use a ragtag, occasionally disinterested, often confused band of misfits who aren't even fully sure that Jesus is who he says he is. It's hard to imagine, that is, until we've read the Gospels. Then we begin to realize the extraordinary feats God can accomplish through ordinary people.

The NRSV rendering of Ephesians 4:11-12 reads, "The gifts he gave were that some would be apostles, some prophets, some evangelists, some pastors and teachers, *to equip the saints* for the work of ministry" (emphasis added). I always smile when I read that word *saints*. I imagine lots of youth workers reading those words and thinking, "Saints, huh? Well, isn't that nice? Whoever wrote those words obviously doesn't know *our* kids. We're not working with saints; we're working with ain'ts! Or maybe if I think about them being used by God, they'd be better described as can'ts. I'm leading Can't-anites! We don't have any saints in our youth group!" It's an easy hole to fall into, but saints aren't stained-glass figures who walk around with halos or hang out in caves. The "saints" Paul is writing about in this passage are the same kids in your group who play Xbox and hang out on Facebook.

This idea that we are born to serve is part of our heritage as Christians. So is the idea that some of us are unlikely servants. We're told in Scripture that all of us, when baptized into the body of Christ, are given gifts that serve the church (1 Corinthians 12:12-31). But then we can almost imagine a smile on Paul's face as he explains the wonder that all parts of the body—even those parts that are "unpresentable" (are you thinking of names and faces again?)—have a valuable role to play (12:23). Peter even uses the language of priesthood to describe our role as believers (1 Peter 2:4-5).

As unlikely as it seems, what that means is that the eighth grade kid who launched a spitball during the closing prayer last week could just possibly be, by the power of God, the same kid who launches a movement of God on his middle school campus. And that sixteen-year-old girl who can't stop talking about boys could be, if she falls in love with Jesus, the same young woman who boldly shares her faith with her teammates on the volleyball team. No wonder Paul writes, "Don't let anyone look down on you because you are young, but set an example for the believers in speech, in conduct, in love, in faith and in purity" (1 Timothy 4:12).

If it's hard to embrace the theological reality of the priesthood of all believers—even middle school believers—then it's a little easier to get our heads around the fact that this equipping emphasis in a youth program is simply more strategic than having a few adults assume the role of messiahs-in-chief. After all, while parents and other caring adults play a pivotal role in the spiritual formation of teenagers, another key force that's shaping the life of every teenager is other teenagers. In other words, one of the best ways to reach students at the high school is through other students at the high school.

That's not to say that adults shouldn't pursue relationships with teenagers, or that we should assume as adults that we can't talk to teenagers about God. I hope I've already made it clear that I believe building relationships with teenagers is central to our incarnational identity. But what I am saying is that *as adults* we're at a disadvantage. We aren't teenagers, and they…um…can see that we're not teenagers.

When I walk on the campus of Conestoga High School, the kids know I'm not one of them. They aren't asking each other, "Hey, who's the new kid? And what happened to his hair?" Now, that doesn't mean that as an adult I can't talk to teenagers about God. I talk to teenagers about God a lot. But it does mean that when I talk to teenagers about God, they sort of hear me with some suspicion *because I'm an adult.* They're thinking: *Of course, he's interested in God; he's old. He's going to die soon. When I get to be his age, I'll probably be interested in the afterlife, too.*

What really speaks with credibility to a student is when the guy who sits across from him in study hall says, "Dude, I know what you're going through. My mom and dad split up last year, and if it hadn't been for Jesus in my life, I wouldn't have made it." Or when a girl gets a note from her chemistry lab partner that says, "I saw your arm today in chem lab. I know what you're going through. I used to cut myself, too. But Jesus is helping me to be healed. I'd love to talk about it, if you want." That's what grabs their attention. So thinking strategically, if we want to reach the campus for Christ, our best approach is to equip the students who are on that campus every day.

Plus, with the legal obstacles that so many youth workers face related to school and campus access, this approach is simply the most workable way of impacting a campus for the Lord. In many communities youth workers have to jump through all kinds of hoops to get permission to be on campus. Our students, on the other, have to jump through all kinds of hoops to get *off* campus. Every single day, they're around students who will never otherwise darken the door of a church building. If we equip the teenage saints to do the work of ministry, they can do it in a place that's extremely strategic.

One more important implication of this mandate for service is this: A ministry that equips is a ministry that multiplies, and a ministry that multiplies is always more fruitful than a ministry that simply adds.

I learned about the power of multiplication accidentally. It was years ago when my daughters were just little girls. My family often traveled with me when I went out to speak, and one weekend we found ourselves, believe it or not, at what was a combination retreat center and dairy farm. How someone thought to combine these two enterprises is a story for another book. (It was an udder success!) But one morning the conference center director/dairy farmer invited me to bring my girls down to the barn so they could see how cows were milked. It was cheaper than taking them to Disney World, and it seemed like a good experience for two kids who'd grown up in the Philadelphia suburbs. So we headed down to the milking barn.

But when we walked in, I think I was the most surprised. I hadn't been in a milking barn since Cub Scouts, so I just assumed we'd find 10 or 12 cows being tended to by a farmer wearing a straw hat and sitting on a three-legged stool, whistling "Old MacDonald." Instead, we encountered a bovine warehouse with row after row of cowage, each animal hooked up to an elaborate system of pipes and tubes.

When we finally persuaded our guide to let the girls actually put hand to udder and milk a cow, it was a little less than I'd hoped. Our older daughter just said, "That's gross!" (She really hasn't liked dairy products since then.) Our younger daughter reached out with her delicate little hand, got a vice grip on the cow, and began to pull— sort of the way a trucker pulls his horn when he's going for a pass. (Five more minutes and we'd have butter on the hoof.)

That's when we were quickly ushered into a room away from the animals, a small room with wires and electronic gear. At first, I assumed this was the command center from which they launched their intercontinental ballistic missiles. But then our guide gestured to a huge wheel in the middle of the room, a wheel on which there were pie-shaped wedges, each one containing a date and the name of a cow: Elsie, Daisy, etc. We were told proudly, "This is our gestation wheel; it tells us when each cow is ready to calve." It was really nothing more than a big cow-clock, a means of tracking each cow's gestation cycle. And that's when, in the middle of his explanation, our dairyman guide made a statement I'll never forget. It was something like this: "When I first took over this farm, I learned a basic lesson about dairy farming. And the lesson was this: Farmers don't make cows; cows make cows."

Immediately, I thought to myself, *That sounds important*, and then that initial thought was followed quickly by a second: *I'm glad the girls and I weren't here the day he discovered this!*

He went on to explain, "I realized that my primary job with the dairy was to produce milk. But of course that meant I had a problem because I don't produce milk. Cows produce milk. And that was another problem because I also don't produce cows. Cows produce cows. I began to ask myself, 'Well then, why am I here? What is my purpose?' And that's when I realized that my job is to feed the cows, to help the cows grow healthy and mature. And if I do that right (I could tell he was getting excited at this point because his words were coming faster, and the pitch of his voice was getting higher; this was like dairy gospel), then *the herd will grow, and the milk will flow!*" It felt like a simple nod of the head wouldn't be enough of a reaction to these profound words—like they deserved a more emotional response, somewhere between "Glory be…!" and "I'd like to invite Daisy into my heart." But I also knew that he'd said something important. As I thought about it later that day, I realized this guy had hit the nail on the head for those of us who want to do biblical youth ministry.

In my early years of youth work, I thought good youth ministry was about growing the herd—filling the trough with whatever feed might draw the kids, and thinking of ways to rustle stray doggies from the liberal church down the street. Who knows—if the program grew enough, the church might allow us to build a special barn just for the youth group! But this crazy little encounter reminded me again of what the Scripture had always made very clear: I am a shepherd. Shepherds don't make sheep; sheep make sheep. What Jesus told Peter, during their last earthly conversation on the beach that day in John 21, was this: "[If you love me] feed my sheep." Notice: It's not "*breed* my sheep," but "*feed* my sheep." It was a ministry approach that took the focus off addition and put it on multiplication.

It helped me realize clearly that biblical youth ministry isn't about wide; it's about deep. It's a ministry burden shared by Paul when he writes to Timothy, his young son in the faith, "And the things you have heard me say in the presence of many witnesses entrust to reliable people who will also be qualified to teach others" (2 Timothy 2:2).

A quick glance at this verse will show four different generations of spiritual reproduction:

- First generation: Paul
- Second generation: Timothy
- Third generation: Reliable people
- Fourth generation: Others

Few verses of Scripture give a clearer demonstration of the profound impact that one person can have by simply equipping a young person (Timothy, in this case) to do the work of ministry.

Waylon Moore, in an excellent book called *Multiplying Disciples*, depicts this principle of multiplication even more dramatically.[17] It begins with Jesus pouring his life into 12 people—one of whom finks out. But then the multiplied impact of that one life reverberates even today.

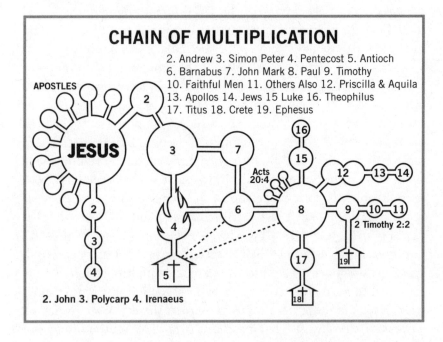

CHAIN OF MULTIPLICATION

2. Andrew 3. Simon Peter 4. Pentecost 5. Antioch 6. Barnabus 7. John Mark 8. Paul 9. Timothy 10. Faithful Men 11. Others Also 12. Priscilla & Aquila 13. Apollos 14. Jews 15. Luke 16. Theophilus 17. Titus 18. Crete 19. Ephesus

APOSTLES
JESUS
Acts 20:4
2 Timothy 2:2
2. John 3. Polycarp 4. Irenaeus

Just think: If there were enough room on the page, I would be in this diagram; you would be in this diagram! The people who invested in our lives would be in this diagram. And the chain of multiplication continues today through people like you. What an amazing legacy!

I remember how as a relatively new Christian, I was a Timothy. I was being discipled by my "Paul," a guy named J. L. Williams who asked me to read a little booklet called *Born to Reproduce*. It's an account by Navigators founder Dawson Trotman of how he began to see the power of spiritual multiplication in his own ministry. (The Navigators started out as a ministry to men in the Navy.) Even today, so many years later, the power of Dawson's words remains just as real to me:

> Twenty-three years ago we took a born-again sailor and spent some time with him, showing him how to reproduce spiritually after his kind. It took time, lots of time. It was not a hurried, 30-minute challenge in a church service and a hasty good-bye with an invitation to come back next week. We spent time together. We took care of his problems and taught him not only to hear God's Word and to read it, but also how to study it. We taught him how to fill the quiver of his heart with the arrows of God's Word, so that the Spirit of God could lift an arrow from his heart and place it to the bow of his lips and pierce a heart for Christ.
>
> He found a number of boys on his ship, but none of them would go all out for the Lord....They were "also rans." He came to me after a month of this and said, "Dawson, I can't get any of these guys on the ship to get down to business."
>
> I said to him, "Listen, you ask God to give you one....Ask God to give you a man after your own heart."
>
> He began to pray. One day he came to me and said, "I think I've found him." ...Three months from the time I started to work with him, he had found a man for Christ, a man of like heart....He worked with this new babe in Christ and those two fellows began to grow and reproduce. On that ship 125 men found the Savior before it was sunk at Pearl Harbor.
>
> Men off that first battleship are in four continents of the world as missionaries today. The work spread from ship to ship to ship, so that when the Japanese struck at Pearl Harbor, there was a testimony being given on 50 ships of the U.S. fleet. When the war closed, there was work by one or more producers (I am not talking

about mere Christians) on more than a thousand of the U.S. Fleet ships and at many army camps and air bases."[18]

Obviously, this kind of ministry takes time. It takes commitment. And it requires a vision that extends beyond the question of how many kids are showing up for this week's meeting. But it's amazing to imagine what might happen in and through our ministries if we were to pursue such a vision. And it begins with a youth program that is building disciples—not just building a ministry, but building ministers.

If you're reading these words and wondering, "Could it happen in our youth ministry? Could we build a ministry that focuses on equipping students to serve?" The answer is *yes!* But remember that it begins with the focus on a few *reliable* people. It's not about how big your ministry is; that's addition. It's about how deep your ministry is; that's multiplication. Jesus ministered to the masses, but he spent most of his energy pouring into the few.

We want to nurture in our students a heart that reaches up to God. That's first and foremost. But we also want to develop the muscles and instincts that lead them to reach out to a hurting world. Building in students a faith that lasts will always involve building in students a faith that serves.

Essential 3: Nurturing Maturity

"So that the body of Christ may be built up until we all...become mature." (Ephesians 4:12-13)

Based on what Paul writes in Ephesians 4, there are two images or terms that should come to mind when we think of building in students a faith that lasts. And, believe it or not, none of them are *fun and games*, or *praise and worship*, or even *pizza and soda*. (Pizza, according to the always reliable sources on the Internet, wasn't invented until 1889, and Paul wrote this letter around AD 63.) In fact, the two images offered in Ephesians 4:12 come from terms in classical Greek that relate to ship building and construction.[19] It's a combination of terms that remind us that disciple-making is about building—mending that which is broken and making stronger that which has been built. In short, Paul is calling the church to outfit a human being in the way a shipbuilder might outfit a ship to assure that it's seaworthy. (See Ephesians 4:14.) This is the work of nurturing maturity.

As we've noted already, Paul's use of the word *until* in verse 13 suggests an endpoint. So, clearly, there is a goal in this building process. But in verse 14, it's equally clear that Paul is very interested in the actual process of building. And he makes it clear that nurturing maturity is an ongoing work. Like the proverbial exercise of moving half the distance to an object, and then half again, and then half again, we never *fully* arrive at maturity (Philippians 3:12-14).

So when we say, as we did earlier in this chapter, that there is no true conversion without discipleship, we're talking about a progressive work, a long-term process of growth and maturity. Even when it follows a genuine birth, genuine growth takes time. And this maturity comes as the outgrowth of God's infilling. We see all three of these elements—the process, the outgrowth, and the infilling—in another familiar passage from the apostle Paul: "*Continue* to *work out* your salvation with fear and trembling, for it is God who *works in* you to will and to act in order to fulfill his good purpose" (Philippians 2:12b-13, emphasis added). We grow toward maturity with the knowledge that God will complete in us the work he's begun. Where we are is important, but where we're *growing* is more important. Nurturing maturity is not so much a question of *position* as it is a question of *direction*.

Of course, different people have very different ideas about the meaning of *maturity*. For the majority of the adults in your congregation, developing maturity in teenagers is probably a relatively simple idea. It basically boils down to domesticating teenagers— helping them behave like little adults. By this definition a mature teenager would, for example, walk into a room where loud music is playing and protest, "Hey, turn that music down! We could be killing tiny fibers in our ears!" Or maybe it would be characterized by an encounter where one friend sees his buddy headed outside and quickly says to him, "Hey, dude, you're not going outside without shoes and a jacket. You can't afford to get sick. Remember, tomorrow's a school day!"

This probably…uh…isn't precisely what Paul means by maturity. In fact, it's misleading for two reasons: (1) There is far too little evidence to conclude that age has anything whatsoever to do with maturity, let alone a biblical notion of maturity. Just look around at the adults you know—age doesn't necessarily equal maturity. (2) Teenagers who are mature will still be mature *teenagers*. That is to say, youth ministry is not about domesticating adolescents so they begin acting *like adults*—wearing their parents' clothing, disavowing body piercings, preferring quiet evenings, and reminding others to turn off lights whenever they leave a room. Teenaged disciples will still be *teenaged* disciples.

Indeed, Paul is quite clear in his definition of *maturity*. For Paul, maturity involves growing into the likeness of Jesus, "attaining to the whole measure of the fullness of Christ" (Ephesians 4:13). This is a process called *spiritual formation*, and it's based on the stunning promise that we "are being transformed into [Christ's] image with ever-increasing glory" (2 Corinthians 3:18; also see Romans 8:29).

The key Greek term at the heart of spiritual formation comes from the root word *morphe*, a word suggesting not just shape, but actual essence.[21] That's why the Scripture says those who belong to Christ will be known by "the fruit of the Spirit," rather than "acts of the flesh" (Galatians 5:16-25). To cite a source that has slightly less authority, but may be more familiar, let's consider the movie *Transformers*. In the film there are two ancient, extraterrestrial clans who are at war with each other—the *Autobots* (good guys) and the *Decepticons* (bad guys). While the members of each clan all change shape throughout the movie, the bad guys are always bad *in essence*, and the good guys are always good *in essence*.

So spiritual formation is not just a matter of how we behave or whether we manage to make moral choices every now and then. The miracle of God's Story in us—better than any movie plot—is that God transforms us from the inside out, from bad guys into good guys. Good guys who look like the Ultimate Good Guy—his Son, Jesus. *Morphe* is a small word that points to the huge idea that God is at work in believers making us into new creatures—creatures like Christ. We do not yet fully see what we shall become, but we know that Christ is in us. And that knowledge confirms for us the hope of glory (Colossians 1:27). It is this "morphing" into Christ-likeness—we often refer to it as *sanctification*[22]—that is a key element of the ever-growing maturity that characterizes true discipleship.

In Ephesians 4:14, Paul crystallizes this growth process still further by identifying two marks of spiritual maturity.

First Mark of Maturity: Putting Away Childish Concepts about God.

One of my favorite childhood toys was a toy boat that my dad and I glued together. I actually built it by myself the first time, which explains why the flag was stuck to the windows of the pilothouse, and the radio tower stood at a 45-degree tilt and snug against the front right hull (like a car antenna). But later my dad helped me repair and reassemble the boat, and he was able to demonstrate that there was actually a place on the boat for all of the parts I had left over. It was awesome. I loved that little boat, and I launched it during many a bath time. If you'd like to see a picture of me in the tub with my boat, turn to the back of the book—I promise you won't find one.

The problem with the boats of childhood is that they don't weather very well the storms of adulthood. They can't stay afloat on the real waves of tempestuous storm-tossed seas. They're relatively easy to build and repair, they're more manageable, and they're easier to navigate. But the true test of a boat is its ability to navigate stormy seas. In Ephesians 4:14 Paul seems to liken the weaknesses of a childish faith to the weaknesses of a toy boat on an angry sea: It is "tossed back and forth by the waves, and blown here and there by every wind of teaching."

All of which brings us back to a concern sounded in the first chapter of this book: One danger in helping young people assemble their faith is that we'll create for them this nice, neatly glued-together set of beliefs that can't stand the strains and trials of the adolescent years. As we discussed in that chapter, building in students a faith that lasts involves helping them put away childish notions about God and come to terms with the turbulent questions and swelling waves of discouragement that can easily capsize childish faith. But it also means nurturing in our students a heart that embraces divine mystery and a mind that cultivates childlike wonder. Childlike faith doesn't deny or explain away the questions; instead, in the midst of those questions, it grips more tightly the hand of the One who knows the answers.

Please understand, this whole approach to nurturing faith goes against a culture that calls for us to dumb down the radical, mind-blowing, category-breaking, miracle-enmeshed Christianity that says things like "blessed are those who weep," "love your enemies," "those who lose their life for my sake will find it," and "though you die, yet shall you live." As youth workers we often feel the pressure to offer students a more reasonable, ready-to-wear, plug-and-pray, heat-and-eat faith that offers childish toy-boat answers to real-life storm-tossed mysteries.

Craig Barnes, former senior pastor of National Presbyterian Church in Washington D.C., tells a story that perfectly defines the kind of "de-constructed wonder" that sometimes passes as "mature" faith:

> When I was a little boy, I loved to visit my grandparents, who lived out in the country. I was there one night, when I glimpsed a shooting star. I ran into the house to tell my grandmother, who said it meant that if I made a wish it would come true. My eyes grew wide as I asked, "Really?" Then I told my grandfather about the shooting star. He explained it meant someone had just died and gone to heaven. My eyes grew even wider, and I exclaimed, "REALLY?" Finally, I told my older brother. He said he had just studied all that stuff in school, and so he began to explain about supernovas, trajectories of light, and light-years. "Oh," I replied. The wonder and the mystery had disappeared; I was now the disillusioned recipient of the right answer.
>
> As a pastor, I've discovered that when people occupy the pews on Sunday morning, they are praying to discover something that will allow them to recover their childlike ability to ask, "REALLY?" The last thing people need from the church is more information that causes them to say, "Oh."[23]

Putting away childish notions about God doesn't mean we silence God-ordained, eternity-sized questions with neatly constructed, puny, human answers. It means we help our students grip more tightly a faith that continues to sail boldly into the winds and darkness of those hard questions. Youth ministries that build disciples will be ministries that welcome questions, struggle, and mystery.

Second Mark of Maturity: Putting Away Childish Thinking in the Way Life Choices Are Made.

My daughters used to crack me up whenever we went to the ice cream parlor. I watched their little faces pressed against the glass as they stared into this wonder-world of ice cream-filled tubs. And when I finally asked, "What flavor do you guys want?" the answer would inevitably be, "Daddy, I want the stripe," or "Dad, can I have the green?" or "Daddy, I want the purple." So I'd explain, "Sweetheart, green is not a flavor; that's a color," "Honey, stripe is not a flavor, those are colors," and "Pal, purple is a color; give me a flavor." And it was a little sad because they never got it right, and I ended up being the only one who got ice cream.

Okay, that's not exactly true. But I knew what was happening with my daughters. They were being little kids, and little kids often make choices on the basis of appearances: rainbow-speckled ice cream, toys that look like characters from TV, colorfully packaged candy. It's an approach that works fine for a little girl choosing ice cream.

Fifteen years later when that same young woman is making serious choices about lifestyle and faith, it will be important for her to put away that childish approach. Paul observes in Ephesians 4:14b that spiritual immaturity is marked by a childish gullibility that can leave us "tossed back and forth by the...cunning and craftiness of people in their deceitful scheming." Primarily, it is a deceit of appearances, an error rooted in an overdependence on the eyes (Psalm 119:37; Proverbs 4:25; Isaiah 33:15; Matthew 5:29; 2 Corinthians 5:7). Sin, after all, entered into human experience because someone saw a tree with fruit that was "pleasing to the eye" (Genesis 3:6).

To be sure, childish thinking is not just an affliction of the young. But in an adolescent culture that lives by the credo "image is everything," teenagers are extremely vulnerable and easily victimized by *the beautiful lie*: It looks like *freedom*; it turns out to be *bondage*. It looks *cool*; it turns out to be *foolish*. It looks like *love*; it turns out to be *lust*. It looks like *life*; it turns out to be *death*. Youth ministries that build disciples with lasting faith will be ministries where students are given not only a biblical grid through which to screen out the lies and propaganda of the culture, but also the tools of discernment so they can make wise choices in navigating the tight spots and attractive temptations that mark the voyage from adolescence to adulthood.

Discipleship is about transformation of heart and mind; it's about a progressive, growing maturity. Youth ministries that embrace this discipleship mission will be focused on the process of encouraging students to grow into the likeness of Christ by helping them put away both childish notions about God and childish ways of making life choices.

Essential 4: Building One Another in Love

"From him the whole body, joined and held together by every supporting ligament, grows and builds itself up in love, as each part does its work." (Ephesians 4:16)

The great privilege of this construction/equipping process is that we as youth workers are not building alone. God uses the whole body of Christ to nurture the parts of the body. And that amazing truth must be a cornerstone of any biblical youth ministry philosophy. We can't really understand Christian growth and maturity if we don't understand that the Christian life is lived within the context of relationships.

The Christian life is not a solitary adventure. It's not a solo climb. New Testament Christianity involves genuine community— not just sardines packed into the same can, but people "joined and held together" (Ephesians 4:16) through a process of "speaking the truth in love" (Ephesians 4:15).

Biblically, the goal of building up, or the ministry of edification—a term based on the word *edifice* or *building*—is both individual and corporate. We aren't just building individual teenage disciples; we're building the church, the body of Christ "until *we all* reach unity in the faith and in the knowledge of the Son of God" (Ephesians 4:13, emphasis added). Each body part must be strong in order for the entire body to be strong, but strong individual body parts will still suffer the consequences if the body is sick. That's why it's so vital that we focus on assimilating students into the church, the larger body of Christ.

This isn't just a matter of program planning (although it is that); it's also a matter of survival. Research has shown that one of the greatest predictors of a teenager's ongoing growth in Christ is membership in, and commitment to, some sort of Christian fellowship. Therefore, an emphasis on relationships must soak into every nook and cranny of a youth ministry. It will determine what programs we develop, how we execute those programs, and who we recruit as volunteers to lead those programs. Relationships are the context in which Ephesians 4:11-16 becomes a living, breathing reality—a growing, healthy body.

Occasionally in youth ministry land, you may hear someone refer to the one-eared Mickey Mouse. The image sounds kind of gruesome at first, as though Mickey has been roughed up by the kids on *South Park* (entirely plausible). But what it refers to is not so much a mugging incident as it is a missing persons incident. It's a phrase coined by Stuart Cummings-Bond to describe the way many church youth programs, either by default or by design, have become isolated from the remainder of the church congregation (see Figure 4-2).[24]

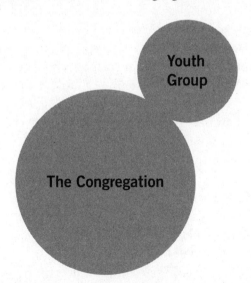

Figure 4-2 The One-Eared Mickey Mouse

Building on this idea, Mark DeVries has described the church as the place where teenagers are "the most segregated from the world of adults."[25] We have unwittingly cultivated a congregational environment in which teenagers are being cut off from the very adult relationships that can sustain them through the turbulence of the adolescent years, and teach them about mature Christian faith. We are, in effect, nurturing in teenagers an appetite for youth group (from which they will eventually graduate), while weaning them from involvement in the life of the broader church that can sustain their spiritual growth as adults. It's tough to build a faith that lasts in that kind of isolated environment.

Of course, there will be the occasional Youth Sunday, and perhaps the once-a-year outing to sing Christmas carols for senior citizen shut-ins; but for the most part, teenagers are missing and "un-missed" from the broader congregational life. And the larger the church, the more dynamic the youth ministry, the more likely and stark is the separation: *youth* budgets, *youth* facilities, *youth* worship services, and *youth* ministry professionals who are assigned the role of nurturing the spiritual lives of the teenagers in the congregation. The implicit message to parents and adults in the congregation is, "*We* are the professionals who know teenagers and have the specialized training to help your kids find Jesus. Please do not try this at home." And parents and adults in the congregation, who often find it awkward and difficult to talk to their kids about spiritual matters anyway, are all too willing to step back and let the "experts" take over.

Everyone is well-intentioned, of course, but the effect is not unlike the overzealous rookie gardener who pulled the plant out of its pot of soil so he could take it into the greenhouse and let the experts prune it. This approach leaves teenagers with a very weak spiritual root system, dying on the vine and wilting under the pressure of post-high school temptations and pressures—not a good result for churches and youth workers whose mandate is to "go and bear fruit—fruit that will last" (John 15:16).

Essentially, what Paul is speaking of here in Ephesians is what Jesus prayed for in John 17:20-23, that the church might be one. Again, notice Paul's words in Ephesians 4:12-13: "so that the body of Christ may be built up until we all reach unity in the faith and in the knowledge of the Son of God and become mature." Indeed,

Paul fleshes out this vision a few verses later when he describes how "speaking the truth in love, we will grow to become in every respect the mature body of him who is the head, that is, Christ. From him the whole body, joined and held together by every supporting ligament, grows and builds itself up in love, as each part does its work" (4:15-16; see also Ephesians 4:4-6).

In practical terms, what it comes down to is this: Youth ministry is all about connecting—connecting kids to Jesus, connecting kids with their families, connecting kids with their peers, connecting kids with other supportive adults, and connecting kids with the church at large. One effective way to evaluate your youth ministry is by asking this simple question: *Are we causing separation or congregation?* Separation is almost always a fruit of the fall; drawing near is almost always at the heart of the gospel (Ephesians 2:12-19). The whole purpose of the church is to help each member individually— and the body collectively—become mature.

DESTINY AND DESTINATION

Over the years my ministry has involved a great deal of travel, and I've come to realize that there are three critical elements that must be considered for a successful journey. Number one: There must be a clear sense of destination—where are we going? Number two: There needs to be a clear sense of starting point—where are we now? Even if we accurately answer question number one, a fuzzy answer to question number two can lead to some serious miscalculations. And for question number three, there has to be some careful thought about how we move from where we are to where we wish to be. This is the question of methodology. As odd as it sounds, good trip-planning almost always works backwards, starting with the destination, then pinpointing the point of departure, and finally, as a last step, choosing the route.

Having taken great care in this chapter to talk about where we want to move our ministries, now in the remaining chapters we'll turn our attention to thinking about the other two elements of the planning process: *Where are we now?* and *How do we get where God wants us to go?*

NOTES

1. Lorne Sanny, *Laborers: The Navigators' Mission, and Navigators Daily Walk Devotional Guide* (publisher and date unknown).

2. Michael J. Wilkins, *Following the Master: Discipleship in the Steps of Jesus* (Grand Rapids, MI: Zondervan, 1992), 75–78.

3. Livingston Blauvelt, Jr., "Does the Bible Teach Lordship Salvation?" *Bibliotheca Sacra* 1986, 143, cited in Wilkins, *Following the Master*, 26.

4. "What is a disciple? A disciple is one who follows Jesus Christ. But because we are Christians does not necessarily mean we are His disciples, even though we are members of His Kingdom. Following Christ means acknowledging Him as Lord; it means serving Him as a slave." Juan Carlos Ortiz, *Disciple* (Carol Stream, IL: Creation House, 1975), 9, cited by Wilkins, *Following the Master*, 27.

5. J. Dwight Pentecost, *Design for Discipleship* (Grand Rapids, MI: Zondervan, 1971), 14.

6. Dietrich Bonhoeffer, *The Cost of Discipleship*, trans. R. H. Fuller (New York: MacMillan, 1963), 47, 60.

7. James Montgomery Boice, *Christ's Call to Discipleship* (Chicago: Moody, 1986), 16, cited in Wilkins, *Following the Master*, 32.

8. Based on a quick survey of the statements Jesus makes about discipleship in the Gospel of John, discipleship involves at least these three elements:

- John 8:31-32—faithfulness to teaching (i.e., obedience);
- John 13:34-35—love for others;
- John 15:1-8—fruitfulness and an intimacy of relationship.

9. Obviously, how these essentials are spelled out and articulated will depend on the biblical passages used as a basis. For example, in *Purpose-Driven Youth Ministry* (Grand Rapids, MI: Zondervan, 1998, 46), Doug Fields draws on Matthew 22:37-40 and 28:19-20 and identifies five basic ministry purposes: Honor (Worship), Discover (Ministry), Reach (Evangelism), Connect (Fellowship), and Grow (Discipleship).

10. Eugene Peterson, *Under the Unpredictable Plant* (Grand Rapids, MI: Eerdmans, 1994), 172–173.

11. Kenda Creasy Dean and Ron Foster, *The Godbearing Life: The Art of Soul Tending for Youth Ministry* (Nashville, TN: Upper Room Books, 2005), 27.

12. Christian Smith and Melinda Lundquist Denton, *Soul Searching: The Religious and Spiritual Lives of American Teenagers* (New York: Oxford University Press, 1995), 266.

13. Kenda Creasy Dean, *Almost Christian: What the Faith of Our Teenagers is Telling the American Church* (New York: Oxford University Press, 2010), 12.

14. Mark Yaconelli, "Focusing Youth Ministry through Christian Practices," *Starting Right*, eds. Kenda Creasy Dean, Dave Rahn, and Chap Clark (Grand Rapids, MI: Zondervan, 2001), 157.

15. Cyril of Alexandria, Fragment 251, *Matthaus-Kommentare aus der greichischen Kirche*, ed. Joseph Reuss (Berlin: Akademie-Verlag) 1957. Cited in *Ancient Christian Commentary on Scripture: New Testament, Vol. Ib*, ed. Manlio Simonetti, (Downers Grove, IL: InterVarsity Press, 2002), 157–158.

16. Vincent points out that *diakonia* ("ministry") in the New Testament is "spiritual service of an official character." (See Acts 1:25; 6:4; 20:24; Romans 11:13; 1 Timothy 1:12; and 2 Timothy 4:5.) (From *Vincent's Word Studies in the New Testament*, Electronic Database. Copyright (c) 1997 by Biblesoft.)

17. Waylon Moore, *Multiplying Disciples: The New Testament Method for Church Growth* (Colorado Springs, CO: Navpress, 1981), 38.

18. Dawson Trotman, *Born to Reproduce* (Colorado Springs, CO: Navpress, 1981), 6.

19. *Katartismon* could refer to anything from refitting a ship to resetting a broken bone, and *oikodomeen* was a term used for construction, as in erecting a building.

20. Kenneth O. Gangel and James C. Wilhoit, *The Christian Educator's Handbook of Spiritual Formation* (Wheaton, IL: Victor, 1994), 39.

21. W. E. Vine, *W. E. Vine's Expository Dictionary of New Testament Words, Vol. 2*, (published without copyright, 1940), 124. *Morphe* is a word that refers "not to the external and transient, but to the inward and real."

22. *Sanctification*, from the Greek *hagiasmos*, means "holiness," "set apartness." It is a word that applies to believers on two levels: One that speaks to our standing, and the other that refers to our state. Our standing: We are made holy (clean before God) in a legal sense by the perfect sacrifice of Jesus on the cross (Hebrews 9:28; 10:10). Our state: We are being made holy in life pattern as we allow ourselves to be transformed by God's Word and God's work in us (John 17:17, 19). One has happened, and one is happening. We've been saved by Christ's death (Romans 5:9), but we are being saved by his life (Romans 5:10). For more on this, see Lawrence Richards, *A Practical Theology of Spirituality* (Grand Rapids, MI: Zondervan, 1987), 22ff.

23. M. Craig Barnes, *Sacred Thirst* (Grand Rapids, MI: Zondervan, 2001), 36.

24. Stuart Cummings-Bond, "The One-Eared Mickey Mouse," *YouthWorker Journal* (Fall, 1989), 76.

25. Mark DeVries, *Family-Based Youth Ministry* (Downers Grove, IL: InterVarsity Press, 1994), 41.

CHAPTER 5

A BLUEPRINT FOR BUILDING

Several years ago, the *Providence Journal* ran a story under the headline, "Big Names to Have Dirty Linen Aired."[1] The article detailed the results of a study conducted by the state of Massachusetts examining cases in which state funds may have been poorly used. Ironically, the study itself, a two-year project of a special commission, cost the state $1.5 million. We're always shocked, of course, to discover that the government has misspent our tax dollars. But the findings of the audit were *almost* amusing (unless, of course, you're a Massachusetts taxpayer). By the time the report came out, there were a lot of red-faced public servants running for cover.

Among the literally hundreds of case studies were these highlights:

- *The Boston State College (now part of the University of Massachusetts) 13-story tower.* When it was built, it was one of the largest buildings ever built by the Commonwealth of Massachusetts. The top five floors of this magnificent structure were originally intended as space for a library, but the designer failed to include any centralized security checkpoints to keep smarmy college students from casually walking out with the library's books in hand. Accordingly, the five floors were heated and air-conditioned, but unused for half a decade. The Fine Arts facility in that same building featured an auditorium said to be so poorly constructed that one could not see the stage from the balcony.
- *The Haverhill (Mass.) parking deck.* This facility was reported to be so poorly designed it could "only be demolished and

rebuilt." Apparently, part of the problem here was that larger cars wouldn't actually fit on the ramp.

- *The multimillion-dollar University of Massachusetts power plant.* The article simply explained, "It was built too far from the buildings it services"—and could not be used.

It stretches the imagination to ponder how you might respond were you the architect of an unusable power plant. What do you say when you've just spent several million dollars on a power plant that doesn't deliver power? Standing there before the board of university trustees, do you play it humble? *"Okay, guys, we have a little bit of a glitch with the power plant. The good news is: lots of power. The bad news is…well, before I tell you the bad news, let me ask you a question: Could you guys move your university over a little bit?"* Or do you try to go in jovial? *"Ohmygosh, do you guys want to hear something really funny?"*

There's probably no really good way to play something like that. But the moral of the story is clear: Think about what you intend to build *before* you begin building it.

FAULTY BLUEPRINTS

Before we spend too much time chuckling about powerless power plants and unuseable parking garages, we might consider that similar stories could be told of the church. We're pretty good at building power plants that don't deliver power, spending large amounts of time, money, and energy on programs and structures just so we can say, "It's the largest ever built!"—only to discover over time that the program, facility, or ministry we've built is "too far" from the people it's supposed to empower.

It's a tragic situation that recalls some very serious statements made by Jesus: "Suppose one of you wants to build a tower. Won't you first sit down and estimate the cost to see if you have enough money to complete it? For if you lay the foundation and are not able to finish it, everyone who sees it will ridicule you, saying, 'This person began to build and wasn't able to finish'" (Luke 14:28-30).

Our mandate as disciples and youth workers is to "go and bear fruit—fruit that will last" (John 15:16). Just as a gardener carefully nurtures the vines and a builder carefully constructs the tower, so must we in ministry give serious thought to how we build what the Designer intends. The apostle Paul underlines this mandate when he writes, "By the grace God has given me, I laid a foundation as a wise builder, and someone else is building on it. But each one should build with care" (1 Corinthians 3:10).

To build the kind of youth ministry program that will result in long-term disciples, serious consideration needs to be given to the blueprint. When building efforts are based on the wrong blueprint—even if they're done with great skill—the end result is still going to be wasted power plants and unusable structures.

One way to begin thinking about the blueprint of your ministry is to take this short informal survey. Answer yes or no to the questions below.[2]

1. The Smorgasbord Approach

a. Is a full youth calendar one of the main criteria by which you or your leadership team evaluate the ministry?

b. Is great care taken to make certain there's a broad menu of programs offered on a weekly basis (Examples: youth choir, basketball, Scouts, Bible study, coffeehouse, Sunday school, small groups, drama team, clown ministry, dance team, Puberty Anonymous group)?

c. Is the main concern of the leadership to keep the kids "active"?

A yes answer to any of these three questions indicates that your ministry may be taking the Smorgasbord Approach—offering lots of selections on the menu, but no real plan for nutrition and disciple-building. It's an approach that begins with the premise that kids are consumers and that if we want them to consume our youth program, we must offer a wide variety of spiritual and recreational products.

One of the most frequent comments I hear about youth groups—and it's usually intended as a positive statement—is when an adult will say reassuringly, "Oh yes, we have a wonderful youth program at our church. Our young people are very, very *active*." And, of course, that can be a truly wonderful thing. But I have to admit that when I hear this type of remark, I often think to myself, *Well, viruses are* active; *al-Qaeda is* active. *That doesn't make either of them a good youth ministry.*

Nowhere in Scripture is there an emphasis on activity. As we noted in chapter 2, the emphasis in Scripture is always on *productivity.* I'm quite certain you aren't reading this book in hopes of discovering some way you could make your life *busier* or just a few more ideas for filling up the vast amounts of free time you have in any given week. None of us yearns for more activity. What we yearn for, what we pray for, what we're called to, is *productivity.*

In Psalm 1, David likens the godly person to "a tree planted by streams of water, which yields its fruit in season" (1:3). It doesn't take more than a few days spent observing trees "planted by streams of water" to recognize that David isn't giving us a metaphor for frenzied activity. What makes a tree a "good tree" is not that it's active, but that it "yields its fruit."

The Smorgasbord Approach to youth ministry usually falls short—not because it does too many things, but because in the busyness of all the many things it's doing, it doesn't allow time to do the one thing it *must* do: "Go and bear fruit—fruit that will last."

2. The Bright Light Approach

a. *Is your youth program based around a young, athletic, hip Pied Piper whom "the kids really like"?*

b. *Has this charismatic leader been slow to raise up and train other adult leaders so the program will have continuity if and when he or she leaves?*

c. *Do people in leadership ever say something like this: "Okay, granted, our youth leader may lack vision, experience, and spiritual maturity. But he plays guitar; he's got an outrageous sense of humor and massive facial hair; and you wouldn't believe what the guy can do with his iPad"?*

Yes answers to the above questions are a sure sign of the Bright Light Approach to youth ministry—an approach based on the notion that the brightest light attracts the most bugs. And since we want kids to swarm our church property, it stands to reason that we need to find our own resident "bright light."

The Bright Light Approach, especially common in parachurch ministries such as Young Life, is typically incarnational and relational. It's almost always focused on some individual who is willing and able to get close to kids and build significant relationships with them. That's good. And, to some extent, this approach offers a genuine reflection of the way teenagers think. After all, it's a fact that students are often attracted to a program not because of *what* it stands *for*, but because of *who* it stands *with*. Even the apostle Paul seemed to recognize that, for immature believers, it might be necessary to help them follow Jesus by helping them follow someone who is following Jesus (1 Corinthians 11:1).

On the other hand, secondhand follow-ship is a lousy substitute for firsthand fellowship. Following the follower isn't a very good way to sustain long-term faithfulness. Plus, it tends to breed a commitment driven more by the personality of the leader than the reality of biblical truth. In environments where charisma trumps content, truth tends to take a backseat. When such a mindset seeps into the church, it can only do us harm.

Perhaps the biggest concern with this approach is that it tends to balance the ministry on the shoulders of one person—which is kind of risky, unless that one person is Jesus. As leaders we all tend to reproduce not only our strengths, but also our own weaknesses. Without the balance of a team of people, it's easy for students to focus more on a human being and less on God.

The Bright Light Approach to programming tends to breed mavericks and lone rangers—individuals who tend to shine better and brighter when working alone. That means it will be very difficult to develop any kind of effective team ministry. And without the diversity and cooperation of a team approach, a youth program will be severely limited in the type and number of students it can expect to draw.

Finally, on a practical level, one of the real drawbacks to this approach is that there will always be a flashier youth program (or school program or sports program) with a brighter light, and many a youth worker has burned out trying to crank up the candlepower. When the burnout happens, as it inevitably does, and the hero/ leader leaves, the entire program usually leaves with him or her.

A program that's built on a personality can fall quickly when that personality is no longer present to prop it up.

It takes more than flash and fireworks to keep kids burning for the long haul. It takes a program that helps students develop a deep relationship with the Light of the World, Jesus Christ.

3. The Bigger Is Better Approach

  a. *Do you find yourself eliminating portions of the program that might have deeper spiritual impact because they don't seem to "get as many kids out"?*

  b. *Do you find yourself asking, "How many?" more often than you ask, "How deep?"*

  c. *Would you honestly say that some of your programming choices are driven by competition with other youth ministries in town?*

  d. *Is your ultimate dream to have youth group meet in the Civic Center?*

If this sounds like your youth group, you may be basing your program on the belief that the more kids we have under the roof of our church building or on the roll of our ministry, the more effective our youth program must be. It sort of makes sense. After all, here in America bigger is always better. Whoever heard of going to McDonald's for a "Little Mac"?

On the other hand, if you've eaten a Big Mac, you know bigger *isn't* always better. If youth ministry is only about numbers, then why not go all out and plan an evangelistic kegger? We've already seen that, in Scripture, the emphasis is far less on addition and far more on multiplication. When it comes to setting youth ministry goals, quality always takes precedence over quantity.

I'm no art critic, but I was intrigued by an article I read in the *Philadelphia Inquirer* about an eccentric artist who was scheduled to exhibit at the Philadelphia Museum of Art.[3] Before Jonathan Borofsky launched his career as a "power artist," he used to spend day after day in his New York loft apartment doing nothing but counting. That's right: 1, 2, 3, 4, and so on. Borofsky said it was an act of near desperation, an attempt to try to bring some order into his life. "Like a mantra...I'd bring all my thinking down to one thought," Borofsky explained, "reducing the noise in my head to one simple, clear, poetic, mathematical noise." As time went on, Borofsky became more ambitious in his counting, filling sheets of graph paper with numbers, one number to a square, 200 to 300 numbers to a page, with numbers on both sides of the paper, changing pen colors occasionally to add an artistic touch.

But, of course, genius often grows out of the soil of adversity, and so it was with Borofsky. One day, during an argument with his girlfriend, the sheets with the first 20,000 numbers were destroyed. Ouch! Four months of work down the tubes! On another occasion, a stroke of creative genius led him to begin affixing minus signs to the numbers, a whim that took him all the way back to minus 12,000 before he regained his forward motion. The most interesting part of this portrait of Borofsky was a comment he made while reflecting on the moment he passed one million, after two years of counting: "I thought maybe something would happen in my mind, but nothing. I just kept counting."

It's a perfect illustration of the kind of frustration and disappointment that comes about when the sole focus of one's work is numbers—higher attendance, bigger crowds, constant counting. The tragedy is that this is precisely where so many of us in youth ministry place our bets. Like David, we number the troops hoping for a sense that surely God is blessing this enterprise (2 Samuel 24:10). And like Borofsky, we expect that at some point *something* will happen—"but nothing." Tragically, and also like Borofsky, a lot of youth ministries just keep counting.

That's not to say that numbers are unimportant or that large numbers are bad. This is not an argument between *big* and *little*; it's an argument between *deep* and *wide*. On one occasion after I'd shared this concept during a seminar, a woman raised her hand to say how encouraged she was by all this "because we've really seen our numbers drop over the last six months." That's when I realized she hadn't really heard what I was saying. I'd intended to make the point that our goal is to grow the group deep and that, in time, that depth would also grow the group wide. She basically walked out of my seminar thinking, "Well, we don't have very many kids coming, so we must be doing something right!"

The fact is that some youth groups are small in quantity because they are low in quality. Sometimes our groups are small because we're doing youth ministry badly! This is not a plea that we reach fewer kids. This is a plea that we don't get so obsessed with reaching many kids that we neglect to nurture and equip the "few faithful" kids we have. (See 2 Timothy 2.) Bigger isn't better, and smaller isn't better. Better is better.

4. The No News Is Good News Approach

a. When you write up your ministry report, do you ever get the impression that your superiors are skipping the ministry activities part and going directly to the budget portion of your report?

b. On the morning after youth group, are you more apt to hear complaints about the mess than compliments about the message?

c. Are ministry decisions based primarily on protection of furniture, carpet, walls, or lights?

d. Has it been more than three months since any of your overseers (elders, senior pastor, church board, ministry committee) have actually attended one of your program events?

e. Is there a little voice in your head that frequently warns, "It's a good idea, but will the custodian sign off on it?"

If these questions prompt you to answer yes, then your ministry may well be haunted and hampered by the No News Is Good News Approach. The tendency with this approach is to focus less on the positive that could happen and more on the negative that might happen. This is a youth ministry perpetually on defense.

The problem with this approach is that it forgets one of the uncomfortable facts of Jesus' ministry, particularly as we see it played out in the Gospels: Ministry is messy, and trying to avoid all criticism is like trying to tend sheep without getting manure on your shoes. We see it over and over again in the ministry of our Lord: Somebody gets healed, and somebody gets mad. A dead man is given life, and the religious leaders want the Life-giver dead. A blind man gains sight, and the Pharisees see red. Ministry happens, and the pot starts to boil.

Why?

It's not because the religious authorities are "anti-healing." Everybody's pro-healing, pro-miracle. It's just that when Jesus healed people, he tended to get kind of unorthodox. He healed people on the

Sabbath. He touched people who were unclean. He colored outside the lines.

Who can forget that sloppy episode in John 9 when Jesus gave sight to a man born blind? It was bad enough that the healing happened on the Sabbath—that's blasphemy. But Jesus healed the man by spitting in the dirt and wiping the mud and spit on the blind man's eyes. Yeeesh. That's not just blasphemous; that's gross! You can almost hear them complaining at the next meeting of the synagogue board of trustees: "Don't we have some kind of mud-and-spit policy here at the synagogue?" But Jesus was more interested in making the unclean whole than he was in keeping the whole place clean.

How many times have we taken the kids away for a youth retreat weekend, and some incredible stuff happens—kids find Christ, decisions are made, lives are transformed. But when we get back, all anybody can talk about is how the church van was returned dirty! I learned early in my ministry that the only way to never do anything wrong is to never do anything. If we start doing authentic ministry in the name of Jesus, we'll find ourselves under fire—if not for violating some major rules, then at least for breaking church policy.

This is not meant to excuse bad diplomacy, thoughtless provocations, immature challenges to authority or tradition, or careless damage to church property. We simply need to recognize that authentic ministry with teenagers is messy. We'll start to attract the "wrong" kids, church carpets will get stained, parking lots may get littered, people will be made uncomfortable (perhaps one of the only sins genuinely recognized in the church anymore), and then, of course, there's the added noise! But if we're always obsessed with avoiding criticism and keeping the ministry neat and tidy, we probably won't build many teenaged disciples—because it's messy work. If you drive by a construction site and it's all neat and clean, that's *not* a good sign. That probably means nothing is being built.

The one really good part about the No News Is Good News Approach is that it's possible to achieve 100 percent success! In fact, a lot of churches have mastered this technique of setting aside a space that is quiet and reverent, with few kids and low traffic. It's called a cemetery.

There's an old Southern proverb: "A dead parakeet always leaves a clean cage." We can build youth ministries that are clean, quiet, always under control, and never over budget. All we need to do is kill the parakeet—just get rid of all the youth! On the other hand, if we see the ministry as a construction site for building disciples, we'd better be prepared to say to folks, "Pardon our mess."

A BIBLICAL MODEL OF EVALUATION

Maybe the best way to approach youth ministry programming is to lay aside all of our concerns about how big, how cool, how clean, and how active our programs are, and begin with a simple statement made by Jesus: A tree is known by its fruit (Luke 6:44; also see Matthew 7:16-20).

Jesus *didn't* say a tree would be known by—

- the variety of its fruit (The Smorgasbord Approach),
- whether a lot of folks showed up to admire the tree (The Bright Light Approach),
- how many people sat under the tree (The Bigger Is Better Approach), or
- whether or not the leaves ever needed raking (The No News Is Good News Approach).

Jesus said it all comes down to the quality of the fruit. So let's think in terms of a programming approach that will help us focus on that goal.

PYRAMID POWER

In chapter 4 we spent some time coloring in a picture of lasting discipleship—thinking about what kind of ministry might be required to build in students a faith ("fruit") that will last. In that chapter we identified four big ideas. Building in students a faith that lasts means building:

- a ministry with a focus on Jesus;
- a ministry that calls students to service;

- a ministry that nurtures maturity;
- a ministry that builds community.

Needless to say, it would be awesome if our students were already committed to these values from the first moment they walked into our youth ministries. How cool would it be if during your opening prayer at youth group one night, some eager student interrupted you to ask, "Can we play with our concordances again tonight and then have heated discussions about theological issues before we break up into small groups to talk about how we want to spend our tithes? Oh yeah, and can I get a new purity bracelet? I gave mine to my girlfriend." It would be fantastic if teenagers came to us as ready-made, ready-to-serve disciples (Baptists would still have to "just add water") who were committed, eager to grow, and faithful young men and women.

But that's not the way it generally works.

Typically, a youth ministry is a mixed bag of kids whose commitments are all over the place. Some are well along in the journey; others are also well along, but they're on the wrong journey. In the average youth group, there will be a few students who are strongly committed; a few more, perhaps, who are moderately committed; some who are neutral in their commitment; some who are moderately uncommitted; and maybe even a few who are radically uncommitted. Some of us may even have a few kids who need to *be* committed before they harm somebody!

The key to an incarnational approach is to meet them where they are—wherever they are—in the odyssey of faith. We've already seen what happens when the power plant is built too far away from those it's supposed to serve. So as you build your youth ministry program, you'll want to think about where your individual students are in their various journeys of faith, and develop programs that meet them there.

One way to imagine those various places of spiritual growth is to think in terms of six different levels of spiritual commitment: Pool of Humanity, Come, Grow, Disciple, Develop, and Multiplier. (See Figure 5-1.)[4]

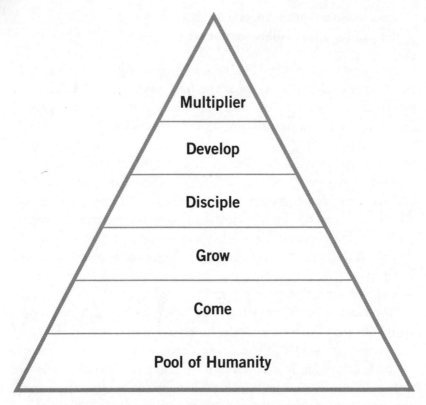

Figure 5-1 Pyramid of Spiritual Commitment

Let's do a quick inventory of each level of commitment.

The Pool of Humanity Level

The first level of commitment is what might be described as the Pool of Humanity. It represents *the entire teenage population within your geographical sphere of influence.*

Every youth ministry, whether it's parish-based, parachurch, or some combination of the two, is located in a particular geographical place.[5] The Pool of Humanity represents the teenage population in that place—the teenagers within your geographical sphere of influence. Your group may not have any influence on these students at the present time. The vast majority of these kids may not even know that you and your ministry exist. But you know about them, and by God's grace and power you want to reach them with the gospel.

Every Pool of Humanity is different. Your Pool of Humanity may be an urban population with several diverse ethnic groups and nationalities, or it could be a small rural community with a fairly homogenous population. It may be a place marked by affluence, or it could be a place haunted by high unemployment and low-income families. There might be a number of middle schools, high schools, and private and religious schools within five miles of your place of ministry, or your entire community might be served by one regional middle school and high school. There are as many scenarios as there are ministries. One isn't necessarily better than another, but they are different.

For example, my current Pool of Humanity here in St. Davids, Pennsylvania, includes at least three or four public high schools within a 10-mile radius. Because of the socioeconomic makeup of St. Davids and the surrounding suburbs of western Philadelphia (known as the Main Line), there are also probably twice that many private prep schools. These are simply facts that must be reckoned with if one is to do youth ministry in this area. Socioeconomic factors, ethnic make-up, the local culture—all of these realities have some bearing on good program design.

You don't have to be in youth ministry very long to discover that what works great in Tacoma or Tallahassee may bomb in Tucson (and vice versa). If we want to see a fruitful harvest, we'll have to give attention to our peculiar ministry environment. Palm trees are wonderful trees, but they don't do so well in colder climates. Jesus basically makes this very point in his parable of the soils (Matthew 13:1-18). The key to our response in this well-known passage is not the seed (the Word God); it's the soil into which the seed is sown. Or, to put it another way, architects don't just start drawing up plans to build a structure; they begin by surveying the ground on which they want to build that structure. So it is when we want to build a solid ministry. Before we construct the program, we give some serious thought to the teenage population in our community. Who are these kids we're trying to reach?[6]

Come Level

The second level of commitment is what we might call the Come Level. The Come Level of commitment is embodied by those *students who are willing to participate in the youth ministry if, and only if, they like the particular activity you're doing.*

Jon is one of those kids who never shows up for prayer breakfast or Sunday school, and he always seems to have unavoidable conflicts that prevent his helping out with fundraisers and work projects. Spiritually, he ranks somewhere between "plant life" and "lower primate," and whenever you "pass the hat" with Jon in the crowd, you're always just a little relieved to get your hat back!

The picture isn't completely negative, though. There are two areas for which Jon has shown tremendous enthusiasm: One is food, and the other is girls. Whenever a youth group activity allows for a large gathering of either, you can count on Jon to be there! Jon doesn't make any pretense about it. He doesn't have any real commitment to Christ, but he does have a strong commitment to having a good time. In short, Jon is a fairly average teenage guy.

There are students like Jon in the orbit of virtually every youth ministry I've ever known. And frankly, sometimes students like Jon discourage us. After all, we're called to build disciples, and it's frustrating to invest time and effort in kids who don't seem willing to get serious about walking with Christ.

But let's be honest: First of all, most teenagers on the outside of our ministries aren't mysteriously born with a felt need for good doctrinal teaching; second, a majority of the students on the inside of our groups aren't seeking this, either. If we target our programming only toward the spiritual heavyweights, we're going to touch the lives of very few kids. In fact, what Paul seems to strongly suggest in Romans 1 is that we are—all of us—natural-born experts at avoiding, denying, and counterfeiting any knowledge of God.

At least these kids *come*. Most teenagers never even show up. So let's be grateful for the opportunity. You can't embrace someone you can't touch. These kids, for whatever reason, are willing to come within our reach! And when we find ourselves frustrated and discouraged, let's remember that every one of us was very likely one of these Come Level kids at one time.

J. C. Ryle, an Anglican bishop of the eighteenth century (1880–1900), says it well:

The ways by which the Holy Spirit leads men and women to Christ are wonderful and mysterious. He is often beginning in a heart a work that shall stand for eternity, when an onlooker observes nothing remarkable.

In every work there must be a beginning, and in spiritual work that beginning is often very small.

Do we see a careless brother coming to church and listening to the gospel after a long indifference? When we see such things let us remember Zacchaeus.

Let us not look coldly on such a person because his motives are at present very poor and questionable. It is far better to hear the gospel out of curiosity than not to hear it at all.

Our brother is with Zacchaeus in the tree! Who can tell but that one day he may receive Christ just as joyfully? ...It may be difficult to see how salvation can result from a man climbing a tree. That's because you see a man in a tree, but God sees a man lost and searching.[7]

Grow Level

Students at the Grow Level are *students within our program environment who are willing to submit themselves to spiritual growth.* They aren't hungering and thirsting for spiritual growth, but they are willing to tolerate it...if food and friends are part of the package! So maybe it's more accurate to say they aren't hungering and thirsting for the Word; they're just hungry and thirsty. They're willing to come to Bible study because of the good-looking girls or cute boys there. They haven't come to study Ruth or Paul, they've come to study Russ or Katie. Oh sure, they may expose themselves to some "Bible lesson" or "small group deal," but they're willing to tolerate the spiritual input in order to reap the payoff of an atmosphere they enjoy. Essentially, that's the difference between students at the Come Level and students at the Grow Level. Grow Level kids are willing to *tolerate* spiritual growth.

Erin wasn't excited about the four group sessions scheduled for the Winter Retreat Weekend. She didn't really consider "the religious stuff" at youth group to be all that interesting. But she was willing to go along because a lot of her friends were going to be there, because there was going to be a ski slope and snow there, and because her parents were *not* going to be there. In effect, Erin's was a Grow Level commitment. It probably represents the commitment level of a majority of the teenagers in most North American youth ministries.

Erin's boyfriend, Peter, chose not to go on the Winter Retreat. He loves snowboarding and he really likes Erin, but he has an acute allergy to spiritual matters. He decided to take a pass. He reasoned that four Bible studies was too high a price to pay, even if it meant being close to his favorite sport and his favorite girlfriend. His is a good example of Come Level commitment.

In fact, wise youth workers will be grateful for both students—for the chance to have some input into their lives. We can be pleased that Erin is at least open enough to "take a chance" on a retreat. But we can also appreciate Peter's fear of being uncomfortable with the spiritual activity that will be a part of it. Incarnational youth workers will affirm both teens for where they're at, while praying and working to take each of them to a deeper level of commitment. One of the stunning traits of Jesus' ministry was his willingness to care about, love, and relate to people not because they'd expressed spiritual interest, but simply because they were people—people created by God and loved by God. Let this same mind be in us (Philippians 2:5-9).

Because so many of our students are typically at the Grow Level in their spiritual commitment, we'd probably do well to take stock of two important realities:

1. Willingness to grow is not the same thing as commitment to growth. Kids at the Grow Level are not seeking spiritual growth on their own initiative. They may come to Bible study on Wednesday night or take part in Sunday night meetings, but only because it requires little more than their passive involvement. We shouldn't assume that every teenager who attends a weekly Bible study is hungry for spiritual food and willing to take the initiative to get it. That's a consideration to remember in preparing weekly Bible studies for youth group.

This isn't to say that we should shortchange Bible study in favor of "fun and games." It is to say that we shouldn't equate presence with interest. Getting kids in the room is only half the battle. The key to building a deeper faith in Grow Level students is meeting them where they are, but then enticing them, provoking them, and challenging them to go deeper. Their presence gives us an opportunity; it does not give us their attention span. We'll have to earn that by speaking to their needs, in their language, and in ways that make sense to them. But at least they're in the room; it's hard to hear from the outside.

2. Consistent attendance is not an indication of consistent commitment. I didn't understand the Grow Level commitment early on in my ministry with students. I sometimes misinterpreted a student's strong commitment to me or to the program as being a strong commitment to Christ. That delusion was clearly exposed for me when one of my most active students graduated from high school, went away to college, and almost immediately made an apparent, conscious decision to abandon any principles of Christian living. Obviously, it was a real disappointment to me, but it was also a real education.

It may be naïveté or just wishful thinking, but it's common for youth ministers to assume that just because kids are involved in spiritual activity, they're also personally involved in spiritual growth. It's wonderful that kids are willing to submit themselves to spiritual growth, but let's not mistakenly assume this means they will automatically, of their own initiative, develop a pattern of continued growth and fellowship for the long term. That's why with spiritual commitment, we always emphasize *direction* over *position* (Colossians 2:6-7).

Disciple Level

Students at the Disciple Level are those who've made a choice of direction—their intent is to move forward and grow deeper in their walk with Christ. The best way to define Disciple Level commitment is to think of those *students who are willing to take the initiative for their own spiritual growth.*

The key word here is *initiative.*

Let's say Erin went on that Winter Retreat. To her great surprise, the most exciting part of the weekend wasn't her friends, or the slopes, or all of the cute guys—after all, Peter stayed home! Instead, the highlight for Erin was an encounter with Jesus. As she begins to share this while talking with her youth worker on Sunday morning,

Erin asks a question: "Do you remember how you made us do the little, like, Quiet Time sheets today and yesterday before breakfast? I thought they were going to be really lame. But, like, I don't know… like, I met Jesus this weekend, and I loved taking that time of quiet to just, like, be with God. And, anyway, I was wondering…I'd like to do something like that when I get home. Um…I mean, has anybody ever thought of, like, doing something like that, that you could do on your own? You know? I mean, has anybody ever thought of doing like a whole book of those things?"

And, of course, Erin's youth worker is thinking, "Yes, there are several thousand of those books…but you don't understand: We won't be doing any more ski trips this winter."

But Erin doesn't care. She wants to grow. She wants to begin spending some time with God. With or without a winter retreat, she's willing to take the initiative for her own spiritual growth. That's a Disciple Level commitment. Now, of course it needs to be nurtured, shaped, and instructed. But this is a pivotal movement in the journey of faith.

We've already examined the kinds of characteristics that one might expect to find in a teenager at this level of commitment (chapter 4). Suffice it to say that the most important quality is discipline. Students at the Disciple Level are willing to discipline themselves to go deeper and further in their walk with Christ. And that's where our role as mentors and disciple-builders becomes so critical. We want to provide these students with the tools they'll need to build a faith that will last. In fact, I wrote this book as a way to offer some of those ideas and strategies. If we fail here, then we've built a power plant that can't deliver power. But when we succeed here, we empower students to walk in the Light over the long haul.

Develop Level

As Disciple Level students begin to advance in their spiritual growth, in time they'll move to the Develop Level of commitment. The Develop Level includes *students who are beginning to take the initiative for not only their own spiritual growth, but also the spiritual growth of others.* We call this the "Develop Level" of commitment because we want to begin to develop and equip these students to become multipliers—students who will dive back down into the *Pool of Humanity* and incite their friends to *Come*, so they can *Grow* by God's grace into *Disciples* who can also be *Developed* into *Multipliers*.

It's important to note that the Develop Level of any healthy youth ministry will include both youth *and adults*—youth who've made a Disciple Level commitment for their own spiritual growth and who want to assume Develop Level responsibility for their peers' spiritual growth, and adults who've made a Disciple Level commitment for their own spiritual growth and desire to reproduce that commitment in teenaged disciples.

It's also important to emphasize that the Develop Level comes *after* the Disciple Level—not before it. I've seen other resources portray this same Pyramid concept in which these two levels were pictured in the reverse order. In my estimation, that's a serious mistake. We already have far too many youth and adults in church leadership who, perhaps unwittingly, have accepted Develop Level responsibility for the spiritual growth of others, but they haven't demonstrated any willingness to take responsibility for their own Disciple Level growth. That is not the pattern we're given in Scripture. (See 2 Timothy 3:10-15.) Remember that Paul said, "Follow my example as I follow the example of Christ" (1 Corinthians 11:1).

This is a particularly easy trap to fall into in youth ministry because we're occasionally confronted with students and would-be volunteers who have all kinds of leadership ability, but all the spiritual depth of a Pop Tart. This is especially common when there is an elected youth council or youth advisory board, since their make-up is often determined more by popularity and status than by spiritual maturity. It's tempting to pass over the less charismatic student who shows genuine spiritual depth in favor of the head cheerleader or star quarterback. But if we're talking about development of spiritual leadership, we need to remember that, "God *sees* not as man sees" (1 Samuel 16:7, NASB).

Multiplier Level
At the final level of commitment, the Multiplier Level, are *students who've caught a vision for going back into their own middle school or high school and starting the process over again, reproducing it in the lives of their own friends and classmates.* When we help kids move into this level of commitment, we're multiplying our own efforts in much the same way that Paul multiplied himself by pouring his life and faith and

vision into Timothy. In the life cycle of discipleship, this fruitfulness is both an end point and a point of new beginning. It is one of the great privileges of ministry.

Let no one think it's easy, because it isn't. But, by God's grace, it is possible.

And it all starts with a big idea: building in students a faith that will last, and building always, resolutely, with that goal in mind.

Before you read any further, take a few minutes and use the Pyramid provided here to think about your own group. Can you identify specific levels of commitment for each of your students? Try to write down the name of at least one student in each level.

After you've been in youth ministry for a while, you begin to grow intensely skeptical of models and blueprints. In some ways, it's like shopping for a car: The design may be beautiful in the drawing room, the lines may be sleek and attractive in the showroom, but the ultimate question is, "How does it run?" That's the question we'll examine in the next chapter.

NOTES

1. Loring Swaim, "Massachusetts—Big Names to Have Dirty Linen Aired," *Providence Journal*.

2. My initial thinking years ago about these various models of youth ministry was greatly helped by Dr. Mark Senter. See his chapter in *Youth Education in the Church*, Roy Zuck and Warren Benson, eds. (Chicago, IL: Moody Press, 1978).

3. Edward J. Sozanski, *Philadelphia Inquirer*, October 7, 1984, H01.

4. There are other ways of depicting this same idea. Doug Fields, in chapter 5 of his book *Purpose-Driven Youth Ministry*, shows these same distinct levels of commitment using slightly different terminology and slightly different geometry. Think of it as the Goodyear Blimp view of the Pyramid.

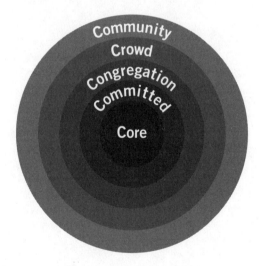

5. Someone might suggest that there are innovative ministries exploring various forms of outreach and nurture in cyberspace, and are therefore without *geographical* location. I'm willing to concede that such a ministry could be viable, but I'd also argue that cyberspace itself is a *place* where kids meet each other and where we might have interaction with kids. It's just not a geographical place in the way we traditionally think of geography. It could still be considered a part of what I'm calling here the Pool of Humanity.

6. This exercise of getting to know one's ministry environment is sometimes called "exegeting the community" (Borgman, *When Kumbaya is Not Enough*). The more technical name for it is ethnographic study. And although it sounds complicated, there are some fairly simple first steps you can take to begin this process. See my book *This Way to Youth Ministry* (Grand Rapids, MI: Zondervan, 2002), 317–322.

7. J. C. Ryle, cited in *Daily Walk* (Atlanta, GA: Walk Thru the Bible, December 1993).

CHAPTER 6
INTENTIONAL PROGRAMMING

Let's begin with a simple premise: For a youth program to be effective and balanced in its scope, accomplishing the purpose for which it was designed, *there must be some type of formal or informal programming that targets the needs of kids at each of the five levels of commitment.*[1] There will be Come Level activities geared to the student who is "not into God at all," but there will also be programs that intentionally motivate the forward progress and spiritual development of students at the Grow, Disciple, and Develop Levels. That's why we began with the Pyramid. It helps us reflect on where our students are in their individual spiritual journeys.

But if we invert that Pyramid—turn it upside down—what we see is more like a funnel. And that's significant, because the funnel shape reminds us that in order to meet the needs of all of our students—wherever they are in their individual journeys—we need a program that is wide enough to engage those students from the Pool of Humanity (it pays adequate attention to evangelism and outreach), but narrow and focused enough to actually bear fruit that will last (it pays adequate attention to nurture and discipleship).

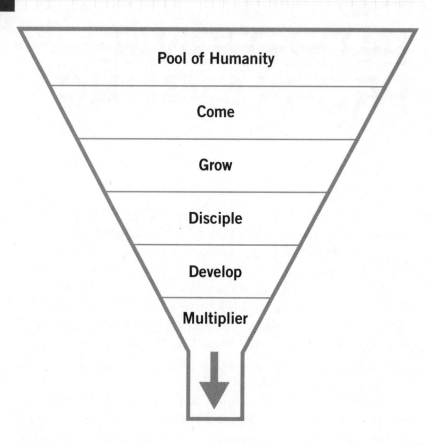

When we picture ministry in this way, it allows us to make some critical observations about productive youth ministry programming. And we can learn a lot about a particular ministry just by using this Funnel as an evaluation tool.

The process involves three steps:

1. **Inventory.** List every activity in the orbit of your youth ministry over the last 30 days. This should include both formal activities (those planned and on a calendar—youth group, club, basketball league, small group, worship team practice, etc.) and informal activities (spontaneous, unofficial activities—going out for pizza after youth group, going to the mall with three girls in your small group, dinner with a family, etc.). Write your list in the space provided on the next page.

2. Examination. Go back and write (on the Funnel) the level of commitment (Come, Grow, etc.) addressed by each of these activities.

3. Evaluation. What do you observe?

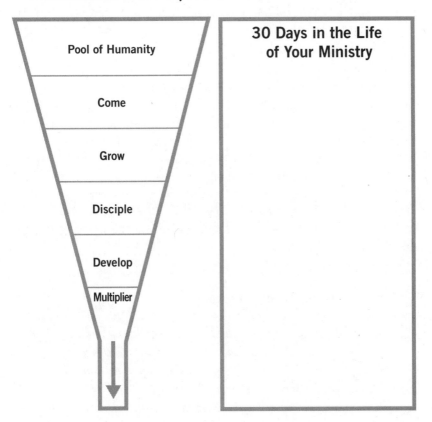

Quite often, when a ministry team follows through on this three-step process, they will make observations like those found below. Let's consider these various findings and think about their implications for building a youth ministry that builds disciples.

OBSERVATION: "We have only one formal program a week, and it really isn't targeted to any one group—it's sort of open to everybody."

This is totally understandable. Because of the time constraints on us and our students, a chock-full youth calendar is awfully tough to sustain. And because we want to reach out to the maximum number of kids every week, we feel compelled to do a program that appeals to the broadest possible audience. Plus, the once-a-week, Sunday night/Wednesday night/Friday night meeting is something of a tradition in congregation-based youth ministry. "That's just the way we've always done it."

The problem with this approach is summed up in the old expression: "If you aim at nothing, you'll hit it every time." Ministries that target everybody seldom accomplish anything strategic for anybody. One simple way to sum up this idea is to think of it in terms of what I call the No-Target, Low-Aim Principle.

THE NO-TARGET, LOW-AIM PRINCIPLE: When there is no intended target group, the tendency is to program for the lowest common denominator.

Consider the following case study:

Jake showed up for Sunday night youth group prepared to lead a program that consisted of a snack, a brief game or icebreaker, worship, and a short Bible study with small group discussion. Had all of the students in attendance been Grow Level or deeper in their commitment, that might have worked out. But after only a few minutes of worship, it was clear that the Come Level students had no intention of owning Jake's agenda. They were in the back of the room, texting one another, and laughing. Then, during the Bible study, the disruptions and discipline problems grew worse. The laughter became louder, the kids more disruptive, and one student, inspired by recent news stories, appeared to be trying to detonate his underwear.

Jake didn't want to ask these students to leave—after all, these were the students he and his team wanted to reach. On the other hand, some Grow and Disciple Level students were really eager to learn and participate in the study, and the disruptions were making that impossible. After several friendly and not-so-friendly pleas for the Come Level students to cease being disruptive, Jake reasoned that maybe he needed to change his tactics and play more intentionally to the Come Level students. He knew that if the Disciple Level students were bored, at least they'd be bored in a polite way; but if he bored the Come Level students, he was worried they might begin taking hostages. So he decided to dumb down the study, making it shorter and shallower than he'd planned. It wouldn't be as meaty as he'd hoped, but what was the point of serving "meat" when several kids in the room, at least spiritually, didn't have any appetite for it? By the time he was nearing the end of the study, he decided to cut the discussion time altogether.

The evening finally ended, but it wasn't a very satisfying night. The Come Level students left the room feeling bored and disenfranchised, the Grow and Disciple Level students left feeling frustrated, and Jake left feeling discouraged and disheartened. He'd wasted a night trying (unsuccessfully) to entertain one group of students; and, in the process, he'd missed an opportunity to nurture another group of students. Because he hadn't targeted his programming carefully, he was playing to the lowest common spiritual denominator. He'd aimed at nothing, and he'd hit it dead-on.

The writer of Hebrews (5:12-13) implies that people at different stages of spiritual maturity require different types of spiritual nutrition (programming). Programming should be designed and branded in ways that help both leaders and students understand what level of programming is on the menu. This can be addressed:

- in the way events and activities are publicized to students (see *Covenant Group* handout, Figure 6-3);

Covenant (Kuv'-e-nant), n. a written agreement; a deed; a free promise of God's blessing; a solemn agreement of fellowship and faith between members of a church.

YOU ARE INVITED to be part of an experiment in spiritual adventure ... not something for everybody ... a challenger ... an exercise in commitment and faith ... a solemn agreement of fellowship and faith between members of Christ's body!

The COVENANT GROUP is simply a group of people who are willing to make a 13-week agreement or covenant with each other that they will genuinely seek to (a) grow in their relationships with each other individually, and (b) grow in their relationships with each other as a group. In the last year there have been a number in our group who point to the Covenant Group as the most meaningful experience they have had in their walks with Christ.

THE COVENANT GROUP

The Covenant Group **IS NOT** some kind of "spiritual Green Berets" or "Superheroes"—it is a group of people serious about making a 13-week commitment to maintain certain disciplines. Basically, those in the Covenant Group are 9th-12th-graders who are willing to make a "solemn agreement" to:

(1) Consistently attend **CORNERSTONE** and **BREAKAWAY** each week. In addition, Covenanters must attend a special retreat (no cost to you) on May 11-12, 2012.

(2) Attend a weekly Tuesday morning breakfast at church before school beginning at 6:30. The first breakfast will be on Tuesday morning, January 24. You will be expected to be at the breakfast consistently and **ON TIME** (please note this).

(3) Practice the discipline of a daily Quiet Time and bring with you each Tuesday

morning an entry into a Quiet Time Diary or personal spiritual journal to be kept during the nine weeks.

(4) Enroll in the "Onward Bound" Program. Information available from Youth Office.

If you wish to make such a commitment or covenant, sign here and return this entire sheet to Duffy. it will be returned to you at our first prayer and sharing breakfast on Tuesday morning, January 24, 6:30.

Figure 6-3 Covenant Group handout

- by making students, leaders, parents, and ministry overseers (elders, senior pastor, etc.) aware of these various levels of commitment and explaining that every program, every activity has an intention; and

- by building requirements into certain upper-level programs so that less-mature students exempt *themselves* from involvement.

Maybe once a year, you should talk with your students about the Funnel—why we have a ministry, why we do what we do, how the various parts of the ministry have a purpose, and so on. I know youth workers who are very intentional about using this kind of language with their students so teens understand: If an activity is a Come Level activity, you can invite your Come Level friends and be confident that it won't make them (or you) feel uncomfortable or out of place; or if it's Disciple Level, you shouldn't come unless you're willing to dig deeper. That's not because we have less care or concern for students whose commitments are shallow; it's because we want to give adequate care and concern to those students who want to go deeper.

Parents should also be a part of this discussion at some point, because they need to understand these ideas too. If I'm speaking with a mom or dad whose son or daughter is still at the Come Level but the parent is eager to get the child involved in youth group, then I'd be totally comfortable advising them that *Activity A* is a Disciple Level activity, so they'd be better advised to encourage their teen to attend *Activity B*.

This is a critical point, and we can't afford to miss it: *Targeted programming is not about the youth leader telling a student that he or she is not suited to a particular program. It's about designing our programs intentionally and in such a way that only those students to whom it is targeted will want to be there.* Having said that, if a Come Level student comes to a Grow Level activity and becomes disruptive, the youth leader must assume the responsibility of (a) not allowing that student to deter the growth of other students, and (b) not catering to that lower common spiritual denominator. That may mean having fewer students in the room; but, again, bigger isn't always better.

Programming for spiritual growth is not one-size-fits-all. Intentional programming will design an event, activity, weekend retreat, or lesson for a target group, and then work hard to make certain those students are the ones who attend.

OBSERVATION: "Our group is really active! Lots of stuff over the last 30 days."

This could be an indicator of a really full and flourishing youth ministry program. Or it could be a symptom of the Smorgasbord Approach to youth ministry. As we discussed earlier, the issue is not how *active* the ministry is, but how *productive* the ministry is. Are we just throwing a lot of ideas at the wall to see which ones stick, or is there some intentionality to each activity?

There is a certain attraction to a youth program that has a full calendar filled with fun, high-visibility events week after week. Once the machinery is in place, these programs are usually easier to maintain. That's why so many youth ministries default to this *program-oriented* approach. Its basic goal is to build a strong program, and—especially in our efficiency-obsessed, consumer-conscious culture—there is nothing we admire more than a strong program. But the passages of Scripture that we've surveyed so far in this book point toward a more *person-oriented* approach. The differences between these two approaches are real, and the choice we make will have a real impact on the nuts-and-bolts ways we program our ministries. Consider the following chart comparing the two approaches:

Program-Oriented Ministry	Person-Oriented Ministry
GOAL is a good program: high visibility, functions smoothly, easy to promote.	GOAL is building people into disciples, "equipping the saints for works of ministry."
STARTS with ideas: youth or volunteer receives mailing or hears of "wild, new idea" and decides to try it with group and see what happens.	STARTS with needs of the kids involved. All programming strategies and ideas are filtered through the question: How will it help us get students from where they are to a deeper commitment?
SUCCESS is judged by function: strong attendance—the more kids in the program, the better; focused on addition.	SUCCESS is judged by fruit: Where are those individuals who've been involved with the ministry in the past? How solid is their commitment today? Are they "equipped saints"?
PRODUCES (potentially) large numbers initially (if it's done well) and involves lots of people. Well-liked by kids; tends to play to "wants" rather than needs. Impresses congregations/boards.	PRODUCES long-term results. May start small and be less impressive in the short run. Usually builds in more "staying power."
PREDICTABLE: Once a "working" system is established that seems to please everybody, no need to make changes.	FLEXIBLE: A program based on needs will change as the needs change; may even necessitate changing a popular program to better meet objectives.

The chief flaw of the program-oriented approach is summed up in another fundamental youth ministry axiom. I call it the Law of Dogs and Ponies.

THE LAW OF DOGS AND PONIES: Ministries that succeed with a religious dog-and-pony show aren't necessarily succeeding at ministry. *What you win them with is what you win them to.*

Just because students are showing up that doesn't mean they're growing up. Great facilities, awesome programming, stunning Facebook pages, creative activities, dazzling worship experiences with disco balls in the sanctuary and a balloon drop during the Eucharist—all of these are great ways to draw in students. But the question is: What are the students being drawn *to*? They may be drawn to Jesus, or they may be drawn to a program simply because it's the best game in town. The problem with that method is that when the students leave town (for school, for work, or for whatever), they might find that the best games aren't played on church property.

If your Funnel is overflowing with lots of activities and opportunities, that's not necessarily proof of a program-oriented approach. But it could be a warning about how easy it is to turn youth group into an activity mall instead of a power plant that delivers power. And it's a reminder that we must be intentional and focused in our program planning. If an activity isn't meeting its purpose, don't expend time, money, and people to keep it running.

> **OBSERVATION: "We seem to have more programming suited to the needs of Come and Grow Level kids. We don't really have anything targeted to the deeper levels of the Funnel."**

If we were to draw a Funnel diagram to characterize this youth group, it would probably look like the one below.

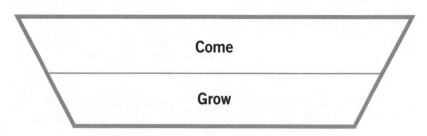

Flat funnel has very little to nurture students at a deeper level of maturity.

This very common pattern of programming is often associated with a third fundamental law of youth ministry programming.

THE LAW OF SPIRITUAL COMMITMENT: As commitment increases, attendance decreases.

We tend to focus most of our programming in the shallow end of the Funnel because (1) this is where most of our students are, and (2) *when we try to go deeper, attendance drops off.* "We just can't get the kids out for stuff like that . . ." The more we ask of folks in terms of commitment, the fewer people will agree to make that commitment.

We've all seen it in our ministries for a long time: As commitment increases, attendance decreases. This was true of Jesus' ministry, and it will be true of ours. Large crowds followed Jesus when they thought there was a chance for free food and healing (John 6:6,26). But how many of those people continued to follow Jesus into Jerusalem and up to Golgotha when opposition grew stronger and the risks became greater?

More than once I've been approached by discouraged youth workers with complaints like this: "I don't understand it. We got forty kids out to our swim party at the lake last week, but we got only seven kids to attend our Bible study on Tuesday night when we talked about Jesus walking on water—and four of them thought we were water-skiing again." I want to smile and say, "Hey, welcome to the world! Most kids like swimming better than they like studying the Bible!" Let's face that reality, understand it, and move on.

What we *don't* want to do is dumb down our program to that shallow appetite. A Disciple Level program that helps build stronger believers may not draw the crowds that a high-visibility Come Level program does. But, in reality, it may be a much more vital part of the youth ministry environment. It's important that this dynamic be understood not only by youth workers, but also parents, pastors, and youth committees.

The Law of Spiritual Commitment also has financial implications. For example, the shallow levels of programming often attract more students, but it typically costs more time and money to be attractive to teens. In fact, you can generally assume that the deeper you go in the Funnel, the less financial cost you'll incur because the deeper you go in the Funnel, the less competition you'll have from the world.

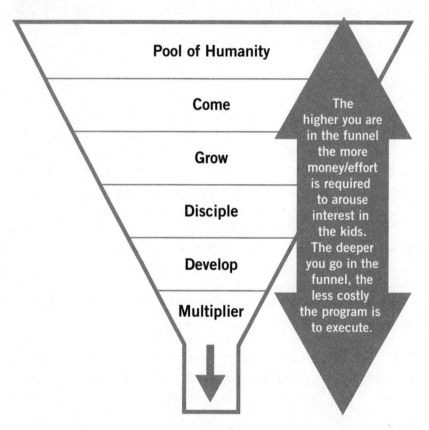

Pool of Humanity

Come

Grow

Disciple

Develop

Multiplier

The higher you are in the funnel the more money/effort is required to arouse interest in the kids. The deeper you go in the funnel, the less costly the program is to execute.

To gain the attention of a Come Level student requires a lot of work. Kids have tons of options regarding how they'll spend their free time, and it often takes a lot of money and effort to give them a compelling reason to choose to attend your program. On the other hand, the marketplace doesn't really care much about kids' souls. When we offer something that will feed them spiritually, we find we're standing in a much shorter line to gain their attention.

I'd much rather use my very small budget to subsidize the low costs of having five students in a Disciple Level program than subsidize the high cost of getting ten Come Level students to attend our Ski Day on Mount Awesome. At first glance, it may not seem wise to put more money and time into a small-group discipleship initiative when, in terms of attendance, much greater short-term payoff—in other words, better attendance—might be seen with the ski trip. But we need to realize that the students and programs at the Disciple and Develop Levels are the "bread and butter" of our ministry. That doesn't mean we shortchange the Come Level program. It does mean that we recognize that capturing geography is not the same as winning the war.

OBSERVATION: "We don't really do anything that intentionally aims for outreach to Come Level kids."

When I was a youth pastor, there was a particular parishioner in one of my congregations who invariably complained whenever we did an activity that she considered to be "unspiritual." And, in her mind, no activity was more *un*spiritual than our Sunday afternoon Ultimate Frisbee Extravaganzas. She complained, first of all, that it was a waste of time; second, it was a violation of the Sabbath; and, third, when I played without a shirt, I frightened some of the neighborhood children.

The showdown finally came one Sunday morning after worship. She cornered me in the hallway and said, "Duffy, you didn't go to seminary to learn how to throw a Frisbee."

Now, let me say that, technically, the woman was right. For the most part, I'd honed my Frisbee skills in college. And by the time I got to seminary, I was working more on racquetball. But, of course, what she was really saying was, "This congregation did not call you as youth pastor so you could teach kids in the community how to throw a Frisbee." And while that also was true, she was mistaken in her basic premise—that the one activity (teaching kids to throw a Frisbee) was completely disconnected from the other (helping students live for Christ).

Had this dear woman understood the Funnel of programming, she might well have been able to understand that *in the right program environment, even the "unspiritual" activities have very legitimate spiritual goals.*[2] Or, to say it another way:

THE IMPORTANCE OF THE UNSPIRITUAL: Sometimes the most spiritual thing you can do is something unspiritual.

After all, the most spiritually intensive program in the world doesn't do anyone any good if students won't take part in it. This concerned mom was right; my job and my vision is to develop Multipliers. But where she was wrong was in not understanding that we can't *Develop* students so they'll become *Mutipliers* if we can't build *Disciples*; we can't build *Disciples* if we can't help students *Grow*; and we can't help students *Grow* if we can't get them to *Come*—which means that sometimes the most spiritual activity we can do with a student is something that's apparently *un*spiritual, something that builds relationships and breaks down defenses. We can never embrace those who remain beyond our reach, and most teenagers will stay beyond our reach if we insist that they *Come* on our terms.

Flat funnel has very little to bring students in from the Pool of Humanity.

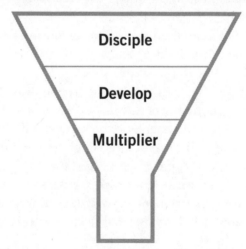

What we see in a lot of youth ministries is a Funnel flattened out like the one in the diagram above. There may be some programming that's vaguely targeted to kids who are serious about their faith, but there is almost no programming targeted for unchurched kids. The danger is that such a youth group can become ingrown and stagnant, a self-focused religious power plant with no concern for those who continue to live in darkness because they lack power. Clearly, that's not what the Designer intended.

DIGGING DEEPER

As you reflect on this Funnel evaluation tool, perhaps you're pleasantly surprised and affirmed by the balance you see in your program. Maybe you and your team have understood intuitively that the gospel calls us to reach people where they are and that the people in our youth ministries are in a lot of different places spiritually. So without intentionally trying to build a funnel-shaped program, you and your team have naturally created a program environment that's wide enough to encourage new students to come and focused enough to nurture and deepen the students who are already there. That's awesome! Way to go!

Or maybe you look at this Funnel model of programming and think to yourself, "Wait a minute; not so fast!" Perhaps there are some elements of this approach that make you feel a little bit uneasy. That's okay, too!

There are some significant questions worth asking here. But at the end of the day, it won't come down to whether this approach helps us build big programs, or well-organized programs, or programs that are easy to maintain, or programs that offer a wide variety of activities. The question will always be: Does it help us build fruit that will last? Let's look at some of the common concerns raised by this approach to youth ministry.

QUESTION 1: "We don't have the time or money to do five or six or seven youth activities every week. I have a full-time job and a family! Can someone like me do targeted programming? Yikes!"

Most of the people who do youth ministry around the globe aren't paid to do it. So any youth ministry model that can't be implemented by "mom and pop" youth ministry volunteers is a model that won't work in most situations. The good news is that it's totally possible to have a well-balanced, funnel-shaped youth program without having to explain to your boss and your family why you have to leave them behind so you can do youth ministry. We begin by reaffirming that your call in youth ministry is not to build a program; it's to build disciples.

If we were sitting together at Starbucks and dreaming about the small group of students in your youth group, I'd encourage you to begin with the Pyramid exercise found near the end of chapter 5—write out the names of the students in your group and think about which level of commitment best describes where they are in their individual spiritual journeys. What I suspect we'd find is that most of your students are at the Grow Level, so that would be our primary target group on a weekly basis.

Let's say we decide that you and your team will plan a weekly Sunday night Grow Level activity for your group. Perhaps it's a 7:00 meeting that lasts 90 minutes. Nothing surprising there, except that you and your team are relentlessly and ruthlessly committed to making sure every element of that Sunday night meeting is filtered through one grid question: "Does this idea/activity/drama/song/game/small group/message fit our Grow Level target audience?" If the answer is no, cut it. This is a program targeted to Grow Level students.

Okay, well enough. But there are about four students in your group who might, if they were encouraged a bit, be ready to move on to the Disciple Level. What about those kids? How can we design a Disciple Level activity for them?

Maybe we'd plan a gathering for these students every Sunday night at 6:00, right before the Grow Level meeting. During that time these four students could meet with a leader or two, and with one another. There would be a meal, some time to help these students grow deeper, and maybe some time for them to share together about their faith journeys. Perhaps we'd call it *Food*, or *Feast*, or the *Pregame Meal*. But whatever we call it, when we post the invitation on our website or Facebook page, we'd make it clear there are some requirements involved.

You might use something similar to the description of the Covenant Group found earlier in this chapter. The idea is to frame the announcement of this group and its requirements in a way that it's truly targeted to students who are willing to take the initiative for their own spiritual growth, *and* that students who aren't willing to take the initiative for their own spiritual growth would opt not to take part—not because we don't love them, but because we love these four Disciple Level students enough to want them to get an opportunity to grow deeper.

Among those four students at the Disciple Level, there might be two who seem to feel a genuine spiritual burden for their friends. They want to grow spiritually themselves, but they're also willing to take the initiative for *other* people's spiritual growth. To meet the needs of these Develop Level students, perhaps we'd invite them to take part in our post-meeting time on Sunday nights when the leadership team gathers for evaluation and prayer.

In addition to the requirements they accept for the pre-meeting Disciple Level activity, these students would have some additional responsibilities. They might be physical tasks (setup, cleanup, take down), leadership duties (lead a small group, take part in the lesson, attend a leadership training retreat, help with planning or evaluation), or pastoral jobs (follow up with visitors, make sure first-timers feel welcome, watch for students who might need to talk after the meeting). It might even be wise to have an application process for students (and adults) who wish to participate on this leadership team. Again, the idea is to intentionally target and plan for those students at the Develop Level so we can equip them to become Multipliers.

But what about the Come Level? We haven't mentioned that end of the Funnel yet.

Frankly, in this kind of "mom and pop" youth ministry context, I suggest that Come Level activities be limited to no more than one to three times a quarter. We've already talked about the demands these activities make in terms of planning, finances, and effort. What's the point of expending all of those resources to get students to come into a ministry that would be badly stretched in helping them to grow? This was the problem of "the old woman who lived in a shoe." She kept having children, but she couldn't feed them. Outreach is important. There needs to be outreach. But it's poor stewardship to spend all kinds of attention and energy on getting new students to come if we can't offer adequate attention to the ones who are already here.

Plus, because it takes more money and effort to do a Come Level event well, it might be wise for smaller youth groups to do these events in tandem with other youth ministries in their Pool of Humanity. Chances are good that several small- and medium-sized groups going in on an event together could do a much better job of reaching authentically Come Level students. Joining together would probably boost attendance as well, since nothing draws teenagers like other teenagers. If we really want to do a Come Level event, then we want to do an event that Come Level teenagers will really want to come to.

Let's not kid ourselves: Explaining a youth ministry program over the course of several paragraphs is much easier than actually doing the prep work, planning the meeting, and serving the students who come. But what I hope we've demonstrated here is that targeted programming doesn't require a massive youth staff, a multimillion-dollar facility, or even a full-time youth worker who can be out eight nights a week. What it *does* require is careful, thoughtful, intentional programming.

QUESTION 2: "Our issue isn't time or money. We don't have the kids! And this Funnel approach seems like something that would require a lot of students. I understand how it can be done with a minimal budget and minimal time available, but what about minimal *kids*?"

We don't need a big youth group to grow kids spiritually; we just need to believe in a big God. John Wesley never had a youth group, and neither did William Carey or Amy Carmichael, but they all grew to the Multiplier Level.[3] So don't let the small size of your youth group, or the lack of any formal youth *group* at all, shrink down your expectation for what God might do through the individual students in that group.

One of the main reasons we get hung up on the size question is because we imagine that strong youth programs have large organized activities with names like *Flood, Crave, Youth Fellowship, God's Posse*, etc. But your entire Disciple Level ministry may consist of taking two students to breakfast every other week where you share about your lives, read the Word, and pray for one another. It may not be a formal group gathering with a name. And it doesn't need to be. Your Grow Level activity may be inviting some students to your house for lunch every Sunday after church. Again, sometimes we're so intimidated by the notion that our call is to build programs that we forget that disciple-making takes only a Paul and a Timothy—and a vision to build a disciple.

QUESTION 3: "I'm not comfortable with the idea of putting labels on kids. Should we really be talking about 'levels' of commitment?"

First of all, the voices we hear in the Scripture clearly weren't timid about this. Much of the language of the New Testament suggests that there are various levels of understanding and spiritual commitment. Consider this sampling of verses:

- **Jesus:** "I have much more to say to you, more than you can now bear" (John 16:12).
- **Jesus:** "As he was scattering the seed, some fell along the path, and the birds came and ate it up. Some fell on rocky places, where it did not have much soil. It sprang up quickly, because the soil was shallow. But when the sun came up, the plants were scorched, and they withered because they had no root. Other seed fell among thorns, which grew up and choked the plants. Still other seed fell on good soil, where it produced a crop—a hundred, sixty or thirty times what was sown" (Matthew 13:4-8).
- **Paul:** "I gave you milk, not solid food, for you were not yet ready for it. Indeed, you are still not ready" (1 Corinthians 3:2).
- **The writer of Hebrews:** "In fact, though by this time you ought to be teachers, you need someone to teach you the elementary truths of God's word all over again. You need milk, not solid food! Anyone who lives on milk, being still an infant, is not acquainted with the teaching about righteousness. But solid food is for the mature, who by constant use have trained themselves to distinguish good from evil. Therefore let us move beyond the elementary teachings about Christ and be taken forward to maturity..." (Hebrews 5:12–6:1).

Secondly, we aren't "putting labels" on kids. We're putting labels on the various levels of commitment. It's ultimately the students who assign these labels to themselves when they decide they will or won't be involved in a particular activity because of what it requires of them.

It's true that during the planning process—when we work through the Pyramid and write the names of teens at various levels of commitment—we are, to some extent, "putting labels" on students. But, to use Paul's terminology, this is only so we can make certain that we serve solid food to those who can eat it. We're certainly not going to make a big poster of this Pyramid and tape it to the wall of the youth room. ("Yeah, Billy, we had to write your name way down there on the wall underneath the chart. See, it's called the Demon Possession Level.") And we readily recognize that God is at work in students in ways that we don't understand—often long before we even suspect it. We can help all the parties involved think more authentically about these questions of commitment when we make it absolutely clear that regardless of any student's current level of commitment, we'll seek to love each student wherever he or she is, knowing that God also loves them all wherever they are now.

Bottom line: Labels are helpful when intention is important. That's why we label medicines, automobile consoles, and grade levels in school—because we recognize that there *are* differences and that paying attention to those differences can help us provide better care (medicines), navigate properly (automobile consoles), and provide appropriate instruction (grade levels in school). If offering that kind of specialized care in the spiritual life makes us uncomfortable, it can only be because we underestimate the importance of intention.

QUESTION 4: "I've heard that some youth workers believe the funnel approach to youth ministry is outdated. Isn't the funnel dead?"

In a recent blog entry, Mark DeVries, one of my youth ministry heroes, wondered out loud if the funnel is passé, outmoded in today's youth ministry environment:

> The kids I work with are just as likely to make their first connection with our ministry in a "deep" Bible study setting as they are to enter

through traditional, large group, high energy programming. In other words, the type of program new kids are most likely to come to is no longer predictable. The most committed kids may actually like our traditional youth group more than outsiders ever would.

Our kids no longer seem to be moving in a linear way through our program (dang it), from "come" to "grow" to "lead." Most choose to plug in a) where their friends are, and b) where they leave with the indefinable sense that it was "worth it."[4]

The question suggested by these comments is a good one. In fact, I agree with Mark's observation that "the type of program new kids are most likely to come to is no longer predictable." Perhaps where we disagree is that I don't think this is anything new. This has always been the case. Spiritual growth has always been unpredictable, non-linear, and easier to diagram than to predict (for evidence, just read Romans 6, or do a biographical study of Peter).

The key concern of the funnel is not predicting where and when kids will encounter Christ; it's providing the kind of environment that might best allow different kids to encounter Christ given where they are in their individual spiritual journeys. The primary emphasis behind a funnel approach, or what Doug Fields describes as a *purpose-driven* approach with its concentric circles, is to **focus intentionally on students at varying levels of commitment.** Rather than a scattered approach to programming that says, "Let's just throw a bunch of programs at the kids, because it's kind of unpredictable," the funnel approach proposes a more directed strategy.

That's not to say God is confined to funnels and concentric circles. If you go hunting, it's totally possible that you might aim at a rabbit and wind up hitting a buck (remember, it's just an illustration, animal lovers).[5] But wouldn't it make more sense to actually target your quarry? I'm no hunter, but, (a) it seems like a shotgun approach would waste a lot of firepower, and (b)—again, please forgive my inexperience—I would think you're more likely to hit what you aim at. My concern is to address the large number of youth ministries that seem to aim low (Come/Grow Level) and wonder why they never hit high (Disciple/Develop Level), or aim high and wonder why they never hit low, or—even more common—aim at nothing in particular and routinely hit it dead on.

QUESTION 5: "Is this really biblical? The whole idea of 'The Importance of the Unspiritual' sounds like we're hiding Jesus because we're embarrassed by him. Isn't the core of Jesus' message 'Come unto *me*'—not 'Come and play laser tag, come and ski, or come and eat pizza'?"

First of all, the strength of this question is that it takes us to the core issue: How does this approach look when we examine it under the bright light of God's Word? Every ministry methodology and activity, regardless of how well intentioned it is, must be measured by that standard. (See 2 Corinthians 4:2-7; 1 Thessalonians 2:3-6.) Another reason this question is helpful is that it reminds us that methodology *does* matter. The ends do not justify the means. Having a good, clear ministry intention is no excuse for ministry activities that reflect poorly on the name of Christ.

On the other hand, at the heart of this question is a flawed understanding of communication; in particular, the basic notion that the audience is sovereign. What that means, in essence, is that it isn't enough to have a message and a messenger; there has to be a *willing* receiver. And as human beings, our receivers are badly damaged. (See Romans 1.)

One of the most telling passages in C. S. Lewis's Chronicles of Narnia comes midway through *The Magician's Nephew* when, for the first time, we hear Aslan's voice—not so much speaking as it is singing. In the midst of the mystery and the delight, as Aslan awakens plants and animals with his song, there is one who is hiding at a distance.

> Ever since the animals had first appeared, Uncle Andrew had been shrinking further and further back into the thicket. He watched them very hard of course; but he wasn't really interested in seeing what they were doing, only in seeing whether they were going to make a rush at him. Like the Witch, he was dreadfully practical. He simply didn't notice that Aslan was choosing one pair out of every kind of beasts. All he saw, or thought he saw, was a lot of dangerous

wild animals walking vaguely about. And he kept on wondering why the other animals didn't run away from the big Lion.

When the great moment came and the Beasts spoke, he missed the whole point; for a rather interesting reason. When the Lion had first begun singing, long ago when it was still quite dark, he had realized that the noise was a song. And he had disliked the song very much. It made him think and feel things he did not want to think and feel.[6]

The great challenge in effective youth ministry, particularly if we're really serious about reaching students in the Pool of Humanity, is that some of our students simply don't want to hear what we have to say. Sometimes it's because we make them "think and feel things [they] don't want to think and feel." Sometimes it's because they come to us with preconceived notions about God. Sometimes it's because they have preconceived notions about people who talk about God. As C. S. Lewis points out, "What you see and hear depends a good deal on where you are standing: it also depends on what sort of person you are."[7]

The primary task of persuasive communication is to break through the listener's unwillingness to hear. For a lot of teenagers out there in the Pool of Humanity, it's not enough to simply offer Christ's invitation to "Come unto me," because what they hear in that invitation is not the voice of the Shepherd seeking lost sheep, but the voice of the Sheriff seeking to hunt down fugitives. We see this vividly in the attitude of Uncle Andrew:

And the longer and more beautiful the Lion sang, the harder Uncle Andrew tried to make himself believe that he could hear nothing but roaring. Now the trouble about trying to make yourself stupider than you really are is that you very often succeed. Uncle Andrew did. He soon did hear nothing but roaring in Aslan's song. Soon he couldn't have heard anything else even if he had wanted to. And when at last the Lion spoke and said, "Narnia awake," he didn't hear any words: he heard only a snarl.[8]

A lot of us know kids like Uncle Andrew. A lot of us *were* kids like Uncle Andrew! And a lot of those Uncle Andrew-kids who aren't willing to come to Jesus might be willing to come and play paint ball or attend a lock-in or spend a day at the climbing gym. And it may be that a yes to that invitation will help us draw them close enough so that, in time, they can hear the invitation of Jesus. Our task in the Come Level is to help students overcome that reluctance—to get our students to the point where they can hear the song instead of the snarl.

It doesn't matter what we say if we can't get them to listen. We do Come Level activities for the same reason that mission hospitals practice medicine, agricultural missions run drip irrigation projects, and churches host Mother's Morning Out programs.[9] We want to bring teenagers within the reach of our embrace so we can love them into the arms of God.

NOTES

1. Although we have to take into account the Pool of Humanity as we plan for ministry, we won't count it here as a level of *commitment*. Teenagers in the Pool have zero commitment to the program; they may not even know it exists. So the first level for which we provide programming is the Come Level. There may not be *much* commitment there, but it's a start. And it's certainly better than no commitment or contact at all.

2. Theologically, I'm not really comfortable with the notion of an *un*spiritual activity. To suggest that some activities are spiritual while others are not is to breed an unholy compartmentalization between everyday discipleship and everyday life. Paul's exhortation in Colossians 3:23 suggests that *all* of our activities should be done with God's glory in mind.

3. William Carey and Amy Carmichael were courageous and fruitful pioneer missionaries to Asia.

4. http://ymarchitects.com/3251/is-the-funnel-dead/?doing_wp_cron. Mark DeVries is one of youth ministry's most reliable and thoughtful voices. He's smarter than I am, more experienced than I am, and nicer than I am. Coincidentally, the day Mark published this entry on his blog was precisely the same day I finished this manuscript. You can imagine, I think, how the timing of this could have been a little disheartening. But I think his blog misses the critical point that I raise here in the text, and for that reason, I disagree with my friend on this issue. On many more significant youth ministry ideas, I'm encouraged to say we are kindred spirits.

5. I'm aware that there will be those who disapprove of my use of a hunting metaphor to talk about outreach. I recognize the dangers of objectifying kids who are loved by God, and I'm certainly not suggesting we think of making disciples as scoring a kill. If Peter were writing these words, he might have drawn from the lexicon of fishing (Luke 5:1-11). If it were Paul, it might have been an example from the realm of athletics, farming, or the military (2 Timothy 2:3-6). If it were Jesus, he likely would have drawn from the shepherd's trade (Luke 15: 4-7). *Suffice it to say that in every case there is intentional pursuit.* That's what we're talking about here. "The Son of man came *to seek* and to save the lost (Luke 19:10, emphasis added).

6. C. S. Lewis, *The Magician's Nephew* (New York: Collier Books, 1955), 125–126.

7. Ibid., 125.

8. Ibid., 126.

9. I fully recognize and appreciate that mission agencies staff hospitals and establish irrigation programs for the simple reason that they believe Jesus cares for people and that illness and starvation break the heart of God. I don't mean to imply that their motives are so narrow as to be only evangelistic in purpose. I would hope that any mission agency and any youth ministry is motivated by a passion for Christ and a compassion for those he loved. (See 2 Corinthians 5:11-21.)

Building a Faith That Lasts

CHAPTER 7

NURTURING PASSIONATE COMMITMENT

It's been a good while now, but I still remember the conversation as if it happened yesterday. I was at a funeral in my home state of North Carolina. It had been a wonderful celebration of a life well lived. But now we were back at the church at a reception of sorts—an opportunity to meet family members and express our condolences. It was the first time I'd had an opportunity to speak privately that day with the elderly gentleman standing in the reception line, so I walked over and asked how he was doing. That's when, without ever making eye contact with me, he pulled a picture from his suit pocket. As we looked at it together, he began telling me a remarkable story, a story so poignant that I requested a copy of the picture and asked his permission to tell the story in the pages of this book.

The history of the old, wrinkled photograph went all the way back to World War II when the elderly gentleman was just a young Air Force lieutenant stationed near Tallahassee, Florida. One day on leave, he was walking around downtown when he saw two cute girls. Wanting to find a way to meet them, he came up with an elegantly simple plan. He had his camera, so he strolled over and politely asked the girls if they'd mind posing with him for a picture. They blushingly consented to the picture, and a passerby snapped the shot—a black-and-white photograph with him in uniform surrounded by two lovely ladies. And then, in a move I thought was kind of ingenious, he made this proposal: "Now, if you'll give me your name, address, and phone number, then when I get this picture developed, I'll see that each of you gets a copy."

To make a long, wonderful, romantic story short, that's exactly what happened. But, to make the story even more intriguing, it turns out the two girls were sisters. And when the young lieutenant sent them a letter, along with two copies of the developed picture, only the younger sister wrote him back. But that was enough to spark a three-year courtship that led to a marriage that lasted more than 50 years. In fact, the funeral that day was for this woman he'd loved faithfully and passionately for more than half a century.

On their wedding day, neither of them could know, of course, what their life together might hold. Surely they never suspected that the last 10 years would be lived in the growing shadows of Alzheimer's disease—an illness that slowly and relentlessly led this pretty young women into a dark tunnel of physical, mental, and emotional decay. But a vow is a vow. So in the later years of their union, as the mind and body of his bride faded into the shadows, this man continued to care for her, day in and day out, refusing to surrender their relationship to even the worst of a truly awful disease.

As I listened to this old guy tell his story, and as I watched him look at the faded photograph with such genuine appreciation, I was moved by his absolute devotion—even after years of almost constant and complete care. Then it dawned on me: *This is what it's like to live a life of profound, authentic passion.* I was so struck by this that I risked asking what might have been an inappropriate question—especially under the circumstances.

I said, "Look, if this is too painful—you don't have to answer this question, but I really want to know. I'm a husband, and I want to love my wife like that, faithfully to the very end. How did you do it? How could you love so faithfully and so selflessly all those years?"

I'll never forget his answer.

Still looking down at the picture with obvious affection, I could see his eyes start to tear up, and then he said, "She gave me so much joy and so much love, it was never anything but a privilege to love her back."

PASSIONATE TEENAGE DISCIPLES

It may seem odd to open this section of a book about youth ministry by talking about an old photograph, a loving husband, and a conversation shared at a funeral. But one of our favorite buzzwords in youth ministry is *passion*. It's used to describe everything from Easter week to intense worship. Even in the culture at large, we seem fascinated by passion. We're *passionate* about sports (altogether rational in the case of Philadelphia sports teams), *passionate* about our pets (just for the record: no, I don't want you to email me pictures of your dog wearing Christmas pajamas), *passionate* about foods (personally, I don't eat any foods that end in a pronounced vowel), *passionate* about our technology (okay, I'll just say it: most Mac users are idolaters), and *passionate* about scrapbooking (although not very many of us). And yet, despite all the talk about passion, we're seldom offered a chance to glimpse it up close.

Our culture has shrunk down our understanding of passion so that it fits into tiny packages brightly wrapped in everything from trash-talking to sweaty bodies and heightened pulse rates, to flashing lights, breathless intention, and raucous loud rallies. But authentic passion is too deep and too rich to fit in such a puny frame. The conviction of this book is that if we hope to build youth ministries that build passionate disciples of Jesus, then we have to go deeper and further than what has become, at least in some quarters, the status quo of youth ministry programming. It seems like much of what we do in youth ministry is intended[1] to help kids "date" God—as if the Great Commandment to "love the Lord your God with *all* your heart and with *all* your soul and with *all* your mind" (Matthew 22:37-38, emphasis added) is the equivalent of "liking" God on Facebook. But biblical youth ministry goes well beyond setting up kids to have a one-night stand with God; biblical youth ministry is about nurturing in our students a vow of lifelong, wholehearted passion. Yes, this is a love that invites and enables and involves and enacts; but most of all, at the heart of discipleship is a love that *endures.*

"BURNING, BUT NOT CONSUMED"

One of Hollywood's greatest movies was Cecil B. DeMille's grand epic *The Ten Commandments.* And one of the most intriguing elements of that film was the way DeMille sought to capture the dramatic encounter when God spoke to Moses from the burning bush (Exodus 3). Sure, the scene was a little bit cheesy, and the audio track made it sound like God's vocal coach was a zombie. But give DeMille credit for sensing the pivotal drama in the scene.

From the text, it's clear that what first captures Moses' imagination is the sight of a bush that is burning but not consumed. As the shepherd of his father-in-law's flock, surely Moses had seen plenty of campfires. And perhaps, after years of living in the wilderness, he'd also seen his share of burning brush and prairie fires. But here was a bush that was burning, yet it wasn't consumed. That was what captured his imagination: "Moses saw that though the bush was on fire it did not burn up. So Moses thought, 'I will go over and see this strange sight—why the bush does not burn up'" (Exodus 3:2-3).

What Moses was soon to discover, and what we can readily see in the text, is that this fire that would not burn out was a sign of the presence of God. And what a profound image for us to consider if we hope to build a youth ministry that builds disciples. It's profound because, with even a little youth ministry experience, we soon learn it's not so hard to get kids fired up about something. It's not so hard to kindle their curiosity. The challenge for all of us—the call of passion, the real sign of God's presence—is to ignite in them a love that burns but doesn't burn out.

Questions like "Where are they now?" or "How do we arouse their interest?" or "How can we get them to come?" are important, but they aren't the biggest questions of youth ministry. The biggest questions in youth ministry are always focused on the future: "Where will they be five years from now, ten years from now, twenty years from now? Is this a fire that won't burn out?" This question isn't, "How do we get them to come?" but "How do we get them to press on?" Most of us are familiar with the big rallies devoted to helping kids "acquire the fire," and I'm all for anything that ignites deeper devotion to Jesus. But as much as I want kids to acquire the fire, my youth ministry experience suggests that the greater effort should be focused on helping kids *sustain* the fire, to tend the fire. We don't want students to just date God; we want them to embrace him for a lifetime.

TWO GUIDING PRINCIPLES

While the purpose of this book is more about blueprint than interior design, the practical realities of in-the-trenches youth ministry require us to translate vision into program. To close out this book with only a vision—even if it's a clear vision—would be to stop short of its goal. Even if we add to that a blueprint for program design, we still aren't able to see what the program might look like when it's built. We need to put some flesh on this notion of a youth ministry that builds disciples. How do we take the vision described in this book and massage it into the muscle and blood of a local youth ministry? We'll explore that question over the next three short chapters.

But first we begin with two guiding principles:

THE HOLY DITTO PRINCIPLE: God shows himself to our students through a wonderful range of encounters; there isn't one right way to grow a soul.

It was the Christian mystic Baron Friedrich von Hüegel who observed that "souls are never dittos." Our task as youth workers is to *reproduce* ourselves spiritually, not *replicate* ourselves spiritually.[2] The natural inclination in youth ministry programming is to plan activities that we ourselves would find appealing. There's nothing inherently wrong with that approach, except (1) every student won't experience God the same way; (2) the ways students do experience God may be very different from our own preferred way; and (3) their expressions of devotion that grow out of that experience may be quite different from our own means of expression. If we aren't aware of this, then we run the risk of helping teenagers grow into *our* likeness, rather than the likeness of Christ.

Temperamentally speaking, some of us are predisposed to action, so we express our devotion to God through missions, service, and getting out there on the cutting edge of hands-on ministry. Some of us are deeply moved and draw closer to Christ through music and dance. For others of us, putting on tights and attempting graceful leaps and twirls just isn't going to...well, let's just say it probably wouldn't move people to *worship*. Some of us are drawn to quiet, contemplative ways of devotion. For others, quiet contemplation is usually one stop on a short journey from quiet time to eyes closed to resting in Christ to *involuntary* prayer to REM sleep. We needn't feel bad about this or be concerned that we're somehow devotionally impaired. Yes, we're all called to do to acts of service and live out radical obedience. And, certainly, we all need to carve out for ourselves times of quiet for prayer, meditation, and reflection. These and many other disciplines form us spiritually. But some of this is also just a matter of temperament.

Gary Thomas, the director of the Center for Evangelical Spirituality in Bellingham, Washington, has identified nine different sacred pathways—what might be described as "devotional predispositions"—through which we can nurture a relationship with Christ.[3] (See Figure 7-1.)

Figure 7-1 Gary Thomas identifies nine different "sacred pathways."

Let's be clear about this: Thomas isn't suggesting, nor am I, that there are different ways to *get to* God. "There is one God and one mediator between God and mankind, the man Christ Jesus" (1 Timothy 2:5). Jesus alone is *the* one Way, *the* one Truth, and *the* one Life; no one gets to the Father except through him (John 14:6). But it's quite another thing altogether to say that there are different ways of developing intimacy with the one Christ who is our sole Mediator.

For a full description of all nine *sacred pathways* identified by Thomas, you can check out his book by that title or his website (*http.garythomas.com*). But for purposes of program design, I think it's practical to break the nine pathways into three broad categories of God-encounters—knowing, doing, and feeling.[4]

- **KNOWING:** *Some students will be more disposed to spiritual growth through gaining knowledge.* Call it a Berean spirit: "They received the message with great eagerness and examined the

Scriptures every day to see if what Paul said was true" (Acts 17:11). These are the students who never miss a Bible study; they even take notes and ask why you skipped the blank on page seven of your outline. Or, better yet, they ask you for a copy of the outline from the study they missed several weeks ago. In short, these are every seminary graduate's dream kids. But you may have noticed that there aren't too many teenagers who fall into this category; this doesn't tend to be the sweet spot of spiritual growth for most middle and high school students. But they're out there. Recently, I was speaking at a summer camp in Panama City, Florida, and a 16-year-old guy approached me after a session. He said he'd "been thinking a lot about Hebrews 10:27," and he wanted to know what it meant! How many high school kids even know there *is* a book of Hebrews? But there he was, and you could sense: Here's a kid who, when you stir his mind, it ignites his faith.[5]

- **DOING:** *Some students will be more disposed to spiritual growth through acts of mercy and service.* These students are the first to sign up for mission trips and get involved in service projects. They invite you to join causes on Facebook, are eager participants on ministry teams (worship, production, drama, hospitality), and annoy you by asking why there aren't more recycle bins in the youth room—and, by the way, "Why do you insist on using paper handouts and flyers that are killing our few remaining trees?" These kids might challenge you, but they also inspire you and encourage you. They have an activist's heart. They want to address everything from child prostitution to poverty to malaria to the modern-day slave trade, and they're looking for ways to change the world in the name of Jesus. Praise God for "ordinary radicals"![6]

- **FEELING:** *Some students will be more disposed to spiritual growth through contemplative disciplines and corporate worship (prayer, journaling, group singing, meditation).* For these students, the organ through which they hear God most clearly is the heart. A faith they can't *feel* is likely to be a faith they consider unreal. We'll want to offer them opportunities of God-engagement by planning group-sharing experiences, candlelight services, creative liturgies, and innovative prayer practices. These kids don't want to just learn new truth about God; they want to soak in it, savor it, and *experience it.*[7]

None of this means, of course, that we should try to craft some kind of "have-it-your-way" discipleship program. From earlier chapters where we talked about discipleship and spiritual growth, I hope it's clear that holistic maturity leads us to encounter Christ in all three ways. To say otherwise forces us to conclude that it's somehow more *spiritual* for teenagers:

- to encounter God through a Bible study than through a mission trip, or
- to hear God's voice through the liturgy than through the sermon, or
- to be moved by a doctrinal study than a worship experience, or
- to sense God's presence through Holy Communion than through a work project, or
- to engage with God through a candlelight service than through a really powerful campfire talk.

Scripture suggests to us that all of these programming elements can be legitimate and important means of grace. Consider, for example:

- **Romans 10:17**—"Faith comes from *hearing the message...*" (Knowing)
- **Galatians 6:9**—"Let us not become weary in *doing good...*" (Doing)
- **Psalm 34:8**—"*Taste and see* that the Lord is good..." (Feeling)

We're left with two important implications for discipleship youth ministry: (1) One person's pursuit of God may not look like another person's pursuit of God. That's not to say that everyone is equally pursuing God, or that every pursuit of God is valid. (You'll notice that smoking peyote and chanting in an altered state didn't make Thomas's *Sacred Pathways* chart.) It's simply to affirm that our students are all wired differently and that souls are grown in different ways. (2) If our ministries are shaped only by our own personal devotional predisposi-tions, we're going to end up starving out a lot of students whose sacred pathways are different from our own.

THE BALLROOM DANCING PRINCIPLE: Discipleship is about helping students stop focusing on their feet and start focusing on their fellowship with Jesus.

When I was in middle school, seventh graders were required to take dance lessons as part of gym class. Needless to say, we knew this was an abomination. After all, gym time was about being outside on the field, running around, throwing objects at one another, and building character. Plus, the gym teachers expected us guys to dance with girls(!)—an unavoidable hazard that led to some of the most awkward moments of my young life. Most of us guys were still con-vinced that girls had cooties; it wasn't until a year or so later that we all agreed we actually *liked* cooties.

You can imagine the passion in the air when the gym teachers called on five of us guys and instructed us to ask five of our female classmates to be our dance partners. It wasn't exactly a scene out of Jane Austen. Chivalry is not high on the awareness list of most seventh grade guys. We stalked back and forth in front of the girls, who were equally uncomfortable, each of us looking for a partner with all the tact of a sheik shopping for a camel.

After we'd all chosen our partners, it was time to learn the dance steps. Our main instructor was also our school's football coach—a man with the unique ability to make a waltz sound like calisthenics. I still remember the booming commands, "One-two-three-slide." We were sure that at any minute Coach Whelchel was going to blow his whistle and scream, "Robbins! Take a lap! Sally! Give me five!" It was so romantic.

In the midst of all this, our gym teachers were trying to encour-age us by saying how wonderful it was for us to become acquainted with these necessary social graces and assuring us that we'd soon see how delightful it is to glide and twirl with a partner to the sounds of majestic music. Unfortunately, most of us were so busy watching our feet, we barely even noticed we *had* partners. We were like stick-figure puppets being manipulated by a rookie puppeteer. To us, this ritual of romance and grace was reduced to three steps and a slide. "One-two-three-step, one-two-three-slide, one-two-three-get off your partner's foot." To this day, I break out in a sweat when I hear "The Blue Danube Waltz."

Perhaps you've never suffered through that kind of middle school gym class ordeal. But it might be a good image to bear in mind as you seek to build a youth ministry that builds disciples, because I'm convinced that a lot of our students experience something similar when learning the early steps of the Christian walk. Perhaps you remember a time in the early days of your own Christian journey when you heard more mature Christians talk about their wonder-ful times of prayer and meditation, their inspiring experiences of Christian service, or their rich times of Bible study. Meanwhile, you were floundering with, "one-two-three-*pray*, one-two-three-*read*, one-two-three-*thou shalt not step there*, one-two-three-*slide*, one-two-three-*I screwed up*, one-two-three-*God's going to find a new partner....*"

One of the worst mistakes we make in nurturing teenage dis-ciples is somehow communicating to them that the Christian life is about getting the steps right. Whether it's learning some new spiri-tual discipline, or being careful to step here and not there, or being wary of the backward slide, we seem to be suggesting—usually with-out intending to—that the key to the Christian life is watching your feet. In fact, *the key to discipleship and spiritual disciplines is not getting all the steps right; it's developing habits that will help us gaze into the face of our Partner, Jesus, the Lord of the Dance.*

As C. S. Lewis put it, "As long as you notice, and have to count, the steps, you are not yet dancing but only learning to dance."[8] Surely this is why the writer of Hebrews encouraged the saints:

> *Therefore, since we are surrounded by such a great cloud of wit-nesses...let us run with perseverance the race marked out for us, fix-ing our eyes on Jesus, the pioneer and perfecter of faith. For the joy set before him endured the cross, scorning its shame, and sat down at the right hand of the throne of God.* (Hebrews 12:1-2)

Notice the emphasis: We are to *fix our eyes on Jesus*. Do the steps matter? Of course they do. We want to be very careful to follow Jesus' lead (1 Peter 2:21). But maturity comes not by focusing on the feet, but by focusing on the fellowship. It always grows from the heart down, not from the feet up. As we help young people grow in their intimacy with Jesus, in their ability to keep their eyes fixed on him, it *will* begin to impact their feet. But sanctification (growing into the likeness of Christ) always happens from the inside out (Romans 12:2).

Nurturing lasting passion in our students is about helping kids learn the dance of faith, not because learning the steps is a big deal, but because these steps can help sustain and nurture the fire of devotion. To translate that into the language of youth ministry programming: The focus of all our teaching, all our activities, all our relational time, all that follows in the rest of this chapter—from the top of the programming Funnel to the bottom of the programming Funnel—is to help students develop a love relationship with Jesus.[9]

THREE MAIN EMPHASES OF SPIRITUAL ENGAGEMENT

To nurture that sort of intimacy, and to do it in a program environment that allows students to grow in ways suited to their own various pathways, we'll think in terms of three main means of spiritual engagement—three tactical approaches that can help us build our students into long-term disciples of Jesus. Youth ministry programs that want to build long-term disciples will be characterized by—

- DIRECTION and not just INSTRUCTION;
- TOOLS and not just TALK;
- MEMORIES and not just MEETINGS.

In the next three chapters, we'll look at each of these in more depth.

NOTES

1. In some cases, it's not even an intention. Sometimes it's just the end product of an unintentional approach.

2. E. Glenn Hinson, *Spiritual Preparation for Christian Leadership* (Nashville, TN: Upper Room Books, 1999), 173.

3. Gary Thomas, *Sacred Pathways: Discover Your Soul's Path to God* (Grand Rapids, MI: Zondervan, 2002).

4. This terminology is borrowed from Rick Dunn's *Shaping the Spiritual Life of Students: A Guide for Youth Workers, Pastors, Teachers and Campus Ministers* (Downers Grove, IL: InterVarsity Press, 2001), 59. Another very simple and helpful way of thinking about these various avenues of encounter is offered in Richard Foster's *Celebration of Discipline: The Path to Spiritual Growth* (New York: Harper and Row, 1978). Foster talks about three main types of spiritual Disciplines: inward Disciplines (meditation, prayer, fasting, and study), outward Disciplines (simplicity, solitude, submission, and service), and corporate Disciplines (confession, worship, guidance, and celebration).

5. If you want to beef up this emphasis in your ministry (and most of us need to), see Barry Shafer's *Unleashing God's Word in Youth Ministry* (Grand Rapids, MI: Youth Specialties/Zondervan, 2008).

6. See Shane Claiborne, *The Irresistible Revolution: Living as an Ordinary Radical* (Grand Rapids, MI: Zondervan, 2006).

7. See John Losey, *Experiential Youth Ministry Handbook: How Intentional Activity Can Make the Spiritual Stuff Stick* (Grand Rapids, MI: Youth Specialties/Zondervan, 2004), and *Experiential Youth Ministry Handbook, Volume 2: Using Intentional Activity to Grow the Whole Person* (Grand Rapids, MI: Youth Specialties/Zondervan, 2007).

8. C. S. Lewis, *Letters to Malcolm: Chiefly on Prayer* (New York: Harcourt, Brace, and World, 1964), 4.

9. Brent Curtis and John Eldredge seem to be pointing to this same idea in their book *The Sacred Romance: Drawing Closer to the Heart of God* (Nashville, TN: Thomas Nelson, 1997): "Instead of a love affair with God, your life begins to feel more like a series of repetitive behaviors, like reading the same chapter of a book or writing the same novel over and over. The orthodoxy we try to live out, defined as 'Believe and Behave Accordingly' is not a sufficient story line to satisfy whatever turmoil and longing our heart is trying to tell us about" (p. 30). They reaffirm this same idea at a later point in the book "Satan is at work...dismantling the Sacred Romance—the Larger Story God is telling—so that there is nothing visible...'to take our breath away.'...He replaces the love affair with a religious system of do's and don'ts that parch our hearts and replaces our worship and

communion services with entertainment. Our experience of life deteriorates from the passion of a grand love affair, in the midst of a life-and-death battle, to an endless series of chores and errands, a busyness that separates us from God, each other, and even from our own thirstiness" (p. 108).

CHAPTER 8

DIRECTION AND NOT JUST INSTRUCTION

In the opening scene of the movie *Jerry Maguire*, a sports agent (played by Tom Cruise) is agonizing over a late-night epiphany that he's lost his way, that he's forgotten why he does what he does, or why he should even care. In response to this revelation, he begins writing something of a personal manifesto. It starts out as a midnight confession, but it grows into a mission statement. Cruise's voice-over in the first scene narrates his train of thought:

> I began writing what they call a mission statement—not a memo, a mission statement. You know, a suggestion for the future of our company. A night like this doesn't come along very often. I seized it. What started out as one page became twenty-five. Suddenly, I was my father's son again. I was remembering the simple pleasures of this job, how I ended up here out of law school, the way a stadium sounds when one of my players performs well on the field, the way we are meant to protect them in health *and* in injury. With so many clients, we had forgotten what was important. I wrote and wrote and wrote and wrote; and I'm not even a writer. I was remembering even the words of the original sports agent, my mentor, the late, great Dicky Fox who said, "The key to this business is personal relationships!"[1]

"The key to this business is personal relationships!" In earlier chapters of this book, we've affirmed the importance of relationships in youth ministry. We saw this reflected on the Emmaus Road where Jesus demonstrated that *walking with* can open the doors for *talking with*. We saw it affirmed in the words Paul used to characterize his own ministry when he reminded the Thessalonians that he loved them so much that he lived among them—that his *witness* was combined with *with-ness* (1 Thessalonians 2:8). Like teaching a teenager to drive a car, relational ministry can be tedious work, even risky, sometimes awkward, and, every now then, marked by honest confrontation. But we don't teach someone to drive by merely giving instruction; we get in the car with that person and give him or her *direction*.

In her book *Practicing Passion*, Kenda Creasy Dean reminds us, "The presence of an adult guarantor in faith is cited repeatedly as the most important factor in a young person's decision to claim faith as her own."[2] In a ministry that builds disciples, we'll want to be intentional about building into every facet of the program opportunities for parents and other caring adults to come alongside students in relationship.

Obviously, these relationships won't all be marked by the same degree of closeness or intentionality. Our personal interactions are naturally limited in scope and in time. It's impossible to be intimate friends with *everybody*—relationships take time to blossom, and we've known some students longer than others. So we should understand that our relational ministry will involve varying levels of interaction with different students. I think about this in terms of three different levels of interaction: the *Contact* Level, the *Connect* Level and the *Contribute* Level. We see these reflected to some degree in Jesus' ever-deepening interactions with Peter:

Level of Relationship	Biblical Example (Jesus and Peter)
Level 1: Contact	"[Jesus] got into one of the boats, the one belonging to Simon [Peter]..." (Luke 5:3).
Level 2: Connect	"Blessed are you, Simon son of Jonah, for this was not revealed to you by flesh and blood, but by my Father in heaven. And I tell you that you are Peter, and on this rock I will build my church, and the gates of Hades will not overcome it. I will give you the keys of the kingdom of heaven; whatever you bind on earth will be bound in heaven, and whatever you loose on earth will be loosed in heaven" (Matthew 16:17-19).
Level 3: Contribute	"Jesus said, 'Feed my sheep'" (John 21:17).

These three levels of relationship parallel the various levels of commitment we discussed in the Pyramid of Commitment (chapter 5). As we go higher in the Pyramid, we go deeper in the relationships (Figure 8-1).

Figure 8-1 The higher the commitment level, the deeper the interaction

Let's look at each level of interaction in more detail.

THE CONTACT LEVEL

Level 1 is when we meet a student for the very first time; we make initial contact. Maybe that contact comes in the context of one of our outreach events that a student attends at the invitation of a friend. Or maybe it happens during halftime of a football game: The youth worker is sitting in the stands with some of her students, when a few of their friends come along. The youth group kids then introduce the youth worker to their friends from school. Or maybe it happens when two adult leaders are having dinner with their small group guys at the local Chick-fil-A: During the meal one guy sees his girlfriend walking in the mall, so he introduces her to the group. Or maybe it happens through a social networking site like Facebook, when a student introduces his youth leader to his friends online. That's the Contact Level—the most basic and earliest level of interaction.

And let's note that, just like in the examples above, one of the best ways to make contact with kids we don't know is by being out there "among" the students we *do* know, on their turf. If we're unwilling to leave the safety of the church property and instead we opt to stay inside our religious bunkers and wait for kids to just climb out of the *Pool of Humanity* and *Come* to an activity, then we probably won't see a lot of newcomers at the Contact Level. But when we do have those encounters, wherever they occur, we should receive each one as a special gift of God, a divine opportunity.

Here are some simple suggestions to help you make the most of that Contact moment.

1. *Practice the discipline of learning names.* There's no quicker way to make an impact on a teenager than simply remembering his or her name. We all want to be known.
2. *Look for ways to serve young people.* Become a coach of the wrestling (basketball, lacrosse, soccer, football, tennis, golf) team, an after-school tutor, an art instructor, a team photographer, a dance team leader, a computer gamer, an Ultimate Frisbee player, or a boxing trainer. I know people who've stepped into each of these roles and thereby stepped onto a bridge that allowed them to make new relationships with kids at the Con-

tact Level. Think of your hobby, your skills, or your trade as a kind of shepherd's rod—a tool you can use to help bring lost sheep into the kingdom.

3. *Remember, the best way to get to know new kids is through relationships with kids you already know.* That doesn't mean we view the old relationships as simply a means to an end. Those known students are important too. But we need to recognize that teenagers are naturally suspicious of adults who seek them out. It's far better to enter the relationship as the friend-of-a-friend, rather than some random adult who just shows up and proclaims he "really wants to get to know teenagers." (It's scary just to type that statement!)

4. *Ask questions.* For most of us, there's nothing more engaging than someone who finds us fascinating. So we need to learn to ask good questions. This means avoiding questions that might put kids on the defensive ("Are you saved?" "Where do you go to church?" "What does your dad do for a living?" "Are you taking a prescription for your acne?") and questions that can be answered with a standard monosyllabic grunt.[3] (If it can be answered with "Yes," "No," "Nothing," or "I don't know," then it probably will be.) In the words of Benjamin Disraeli, "Talk to people about themselves and they will listen for hours."[4]

5. *Don't force your way into social situations where you wouldn't be welcome.* This principle definitely applies in the hallways at school, at a lacrosse game, or at the local Cineplex on Friday night. But you should also be especially sensitive to this with regard to Facebook and other social networking sites. There's a fine line between "salt of the earth" and an assault on the earthlings.

THE CONNECT LEVEL

Once we've made initial contact with a student, we want to be alert for ways we can become for that student what the apostle Paul called "an ambassador of reconciliation" (2 Corinthians 5:18-20). That's why we call it the Connect Level. At this stage of the relationship, we want to build relational bridges—bridges of trust, bridges of credibility, bridges of concern, bridges that extend the reach of God's love. These bridges are built on the girders of *communication* (email, Facebook, texting, phone calls, actual note/letter writing, face-to-face conversation), *affirmation* (everybody needs a cheerleader),[5] and *shared experience* (including both planned and unplanned—everything from a backpacking trip to a bus breakdown).

Remember, this level of interaction is slightly more in-depth. By this time, some water has gone under the relational bridge, and the conversational exchange can be proportionately deeper. At the Connect Level, it might be appropriate to—

1. Ask a student to pray for you over a specific issue.
2. Do a quiet time with a student.
3. Ask: "How is your walk with God going?"
4. Send him a copy of an article about spiritual growth and then follow up by asking for his thoughts.
5. Write a prayer about a student's walk with God and show it to her.
6. Invite a couple of students to run errands with you or help you with a project around the house or an act of service for an elderly church member.
7. Tell a student what you see God doing in his life.

There are any number of ways we can build this relational bridge—some are more serious, some are just fun, and some are simply a creative way of saying, "I'm thinking of you today." The goal is to build trust and earn access so you have an avenue of life-exchange that can lead you to a deeper level of relationship. Here are some simple examples:

Make Your Own Posters
Most of us have seen the kinds of posters that are sold in Christian bookstores: Pictures of landscapes, athletes, footprints on a beach, or cute animals in various poses, and all with a Bible verse or encouraging phrase superimposed. Now, these posters are fine, and they can be a real inspiration to people. But what about a poster customized for one of your students or designed exclusively by members of your youth group? Most printshop chains and many film develop-

ment outlets can take any slide or picture, blow it up to poster size, and superimpose some favorite verse or phrase onto it.

For example, what better way to extend the memories of last summer's camp than by making a poster using pictures you took at camp and superimposing across the bottom: "I am confident of this, that the one who began a good work among you will bring it to completion at the day of Jesus Christ" (Philippians 1:6, NRSV). Or how about a poster using pictures you shot during a youth group work project and this verse across the bottom: "Don't let anyone look down on you because you are young, but set an example for the believers in speech, in conduct, in love, in faith and in purity" (1 Timothy 4:12). Or maybe just for fun, blow up a picture of one of your students taken just after a Mud Bowl event and superimpose the verse, "You are clean, though not every one of you" (John 13:10b).

One neat facet of making your own posters is that after you've had these customized posters hanging on the youth room walls for a while, you can take them down and sell them to students and parents so you can get some new posters made. Try doing *that* with one of your old bookstore posters!

Good Morning, America
This idea isn't very elaborate, but a one-of-a-kind wake-up call can be a pretty unique experience for a student in your youth group. Begin by making arrangements with the student's parents so the wake-up experience isn't more special than you planned! Then, with a video camera in tow (very important), you enter the student's bedroom early one Saturday morning and give her a truly eye-opening wake-up experience.

There are several possible wake-up options:

1. Go to the student's home wearing a gorilla costume so he thinks he's being awakened by King Kong.
2. Wake up the student by using a leaf blower.
3. Go to the student's home with a hot breakfast from McDonald's and a few friends who will serve the student breakfast in bed.

4. Enter the student's room with several other youth group kids and begin singing Christmas carols (this is perfect around mid-July).
5. Give the student a birthday wake-up call by having some kids from the group sing "Happy Birthday" and then share a birthday (pan)cake breakfast. (You might even do this on the student's actual birthday!)

One Sweet Letter

On your way home from work one day, stop at a convenience store and buy a handful of candy —but don't buy just your favorites! Select candy with names you can incorporate into a letter to one of your students. Then write the letter on a big sheet of cardstock (posterboard) by taping or gluing the candy bars and other sweets into the text of the letter as a substitute for written words.

> **SAMPLE:** Hey, Hank! *LOOK!* here, dude. I was thinking about you today and can say that *BAR NONE*, you are one of the coolest middle schoolers in the entire *MILKY WAY*. *U-NO*, I am sure God has great things in store for you both *NOW AND LATER*. Don't let the *NERDS* at school give you a hard time about becoming a Christian. There is a great *PAYDAY* awaiting those who live for Jesus. You are one bad *MAMBA*. With your gifts and talents, God is going to use you for *GOOD & PLENTY* of kids are going to benefit from your leadership. I wouldn't trade you for a *100 GRAND*. Thanks for being my friend.

Letter from God

Many students don't believe God's Word is relevant to their lives and just assume it has nothing to say to them. Personalize a letter to a student by composing the letter with Bible verses. By stringing a few verses together, you can personalize a letter to show a student that God's Word speaks, and it speaks to individual hearts.

> **SAMPLE:**
>
> Dear Earl,
>
> I have created you (1). I have called you by name (2). You are precious in my sight (3). I rejoice over you with joy (4). I called you into

fellowship with my Son, Jesus (5). I want your love; I want you to know me (6). Seek me day by day, delight to know my ways (7). Press on to know me and I will respond to you as surely as the coming of the rain of early spring (8). Come and behold my beauty (9). Pour out your heart to me like water (10). Know the refreshment that comes from my presence (11).

Love always,

Your Heavenly Father

(1) Genesis 1:27; (2) Isaiah 43:1; (3) Isaiah 43:4; (4) Zephaniah 3:17; (5) 1 Corinthians 1:9; (6) Hosea 6:6; (7) Isaiah 58:2; (8) Hosea 6:3; (9) Psalm 27:4; (10) Lamentations 2:19; (11) Acts 3:19

Recycled Stationery

Write a letter to a student—maybe just a quick shout-out or a word of encouragement. But instead of writing the letter on a note card or a sheet of notebook paper, write it on some nontraditional stationery:

- A toothpaste box
- A paper plate
- Gauze
- A knee brace
- A barf bag
- A restaurant tray cover
- A piece of wood
- The bottom of an old shoe
- A toilet seat cover
- A soccer ball

Any of these items, if properly posted, can be sent either "as is" or inside an envelope through the U.S. Postal Service. In fact, hanging on the wall of my office, I used to have a toilet seat cover that I'd received in the mail from a friend who wrote on it: SAW THIS, THOUGHT OF YOU. It has since been replaced by a small handwritten note that says, SORRY ABOUT THE MISSING TOILET SEAT LETTER. I NEEDED IT.

Engaging with students at the Connect Level earns us the high and holy privilege of building into their lives.

THE CONTRIBUTE LEVEL

If the Connect Level is about showing *attention*, the Contribute Level of relationships is about showing *attention with intention*. This is the point in the relationship when we begin investing more deeply into a student. Think of Elijah being a mentor for Elisha; or Jesus investing in Peter, James, and John; or Paul investing into Timothy; or Yoda training Luke Skywalker. We call it the Contribute Level because this is life-on-life transfer, where the spiritual gifts invested are then multiplied.

Frankly, there aren't any easy shortcuts or cute tricks here. A brief study, for example, of Jesus' relationship with Peter demonstrates that this is difficult, exhilarating, discouraging, and costly work. To walk with a student through that first moment of contact ("Come, follow me..."), to that point when it all seems to connect ("You are the Son of God"), and all the way to that level of commission and contribution ("Feed my sheep") is a grand and difficult odyssey. There are no snappy formulas.

That's probably why this is one of the toughest areas of ministry—at least that's what I've observed in working with volunteer team members. Most adults aren't comfortable talking to kids at all (Contact Level). A few of them feel comfortable talking to kids as long as the conversation is about movies, sports, music, and Facebook chatter (Connect Level). But even those leaders who are pretty relaxed in their interactions with students at the Connect Level tend to struggle with moving the conversation to a deeper level (Contribute Level). It's not that they don't *want* to; they sense that the whole point of building the bridge is so that communication traffic can happen. But they have difficulty in those face-to-face conversations that ask the awkward questions and talk about the hard stuff. As a youth pastor trying to build a ministry that builds disciples, I wanted to figure out a way to address that issue.

Let's consider one real-life case study:

Sally is a junior in high school. Two years ago at a winter retreat, Sally made a very genuine and life-changing decision to be a follower of Jesus Christ. In a lot of ways, she's a youth worker's prayer request. She's active in our program. She reaches out to her friends at school. Her daily time in the Word is at a level of consistency that I probably didn't reach until my second year of seminary!

Sally's problem is that she is very weak in the area of personal management. She arrives late to meetings (if she remembers to come at all), and she is generally undependable. Her grades have been slipping at school, and her mom is on her case because she feels that Sally is being disrespectful toward others at home, particularly in the way she forgets to clean up after herself (in the kitchen, in the family room, etc). Her mom is pleased that her daughter reads the Bible, but she'd be even more pleased if all that Bible reading impacted her week between youth meetings. All of this disorganization has begun to affect not only Sally's relationships with her parents and friends, but also the way she thinks about herself.

Early on in my youth ministry, I probably would have dealt with Sally in one of two equally unproductive ways:

"Sally is a typical teenager." I would have shrugged my shoulders and shaken my head, feeling resigned to the fact that "kids are kids" and that as long as Sally wasn't on drugs or sexually involved with some guy, then I was doing my job. My prayer for Sally would have been that "she will grow up and act like an adult." (At the time it never occurred to me that this was precisely the attitude that's produced so many adults who act like teenagers!) I never really thought of Sally's "decision to be a follower of Christ" as being something that would reach into the mundane affairs of personal management.

"Sally needs to be more committed." I might have assumed that Sally "just isn't serious about the Lord." If she were really sold out to Jesus, then she'd be dealing with these problem areas. I might have dealt with Sally by assuming she'd fallen away from her commitment to Christ, or that perhaps her conversion just wasn't *real* enough or *deep* enough.

Each of these approaches to Sally's growing pains represents *two very common errors* related to the nurture of teenage disciples.

Error 1: We ignore the fact that spiritual growth is practical. Samuel Chadwick, a godly preacher of the eighteenth century, reportedly used to pray, "Lord, make us intensely spiritual, thoroughly practical, and perfectly natural." He understood that holiness is not an obsolete monastic discipline unrelated to daily life. Biblical holiness should affect every dimension of our own lives, and the lives of our youth. We've mistakenly believed or implied that having sex too soon is a spiritual problem but slothful living is not.

When the apostle Paul wrote, "I decided to know nothing among you except Jesus Christ, and him crucified" (1 Corinthians 2:2, NRSV), he followed that statement with 14 more chapters in which he addressed a diverse range of practical lifestyle issues. In doing so, he was reminding us that the gospel isn't good news if it doesn't speak to the bad news—and sometimes the bad news is not in the big headliner sins we love to hate, but it's in the little practical sins we hate to give up. I wanted to invest into Sally. I wanted her to develop her obvious leadership potential and deepen her devotional life. But in the process of encouraging Sally to be intensely spiritual, I'm not sure I knew how to help her make her faith thoroughly practical.

Error 2: We forget that spiritual growth is a process. With all our talk about the difference Christ can make in a student's life, we've forgotten that spiritual growth takes time. I like to remind kids of God's words in Deuteronomy 7:22-23—"The LORD your God will clear away these nations before you little by little; you will not be able to put an end to them quickly, for the wild beasts would grow too numerous for you" (NASB). Spiritual growth is a process of attacking one beast at a time.

Like so many Christian teenagers in our youth groups, Sally didn't need to be "reconverted" (whatever that means). Sally was tuned to the right channel; but to make the image of Christ in her still clearer, she needed *fine-tuning*. Unfortunately, a lot of our work in youth ministry seems geared toward channel changing. It's as if we assume the fine-tuning will happen by itself. However, what we begin to realize over time is that if a ministry is going to build disciples of Jesus, then it needs to help students identify and deal with the beasts in their lives.

BUILDING IN TO BUILD UP: THE FINE ART OF FINE-TUNING

Relational ministry at the Contribute Level is marked by some basic premises:

1. Fine-tuning is a one-to-one process. In trying to meet Sally's needs, we might initiate a series of Bible studies about time management, or living in community, or living a servant lifestyle, or Colossians 3:23—"Whatever you do, work at it with all your heart, as working for the Lord, not for human masters." Those are all great ideas, but what about John? He's just as interested in spiritual growth as Sally is, but the beast he needs to attack is a bad relationship with his sister. Or how about Steve—a fantastic kid who really loves the Lord but can't seem to work out his relationship with his parents? And then there's Jan who's experienced years of abuse and has now started cutting herself; and Bob really loves the Lord, but he can't seem to kick his addiction to pornography. The problem with fine-tuning is that the process varies for each receiver. It's not a group activity. So we need to find a way to meet the unique fine-tuning needs of each of the youth in our program.

2. Fine-tuning takes time. The reason we don't give more attention to this sort of ministry is that it's very time-consuming. Fine-tuning takes careful listening. Except in the smallest of programs, trying to do this kind of ministry without the aid of a volunteer team is impossible. To help the Sallys and Steves and Johns and Bobs deal with their problems requires accountability. It's not enough to merely suggest strategies for dealing with these issues. There need to be occasions for frequent "checking in."

3. Fine-tuning requires creativity. It's not so hard to talk to Sally about drugs. There's plenty of material available with various books and studies we can use—a lot of the work has been done already. But youth workers who attempt to deal with some of these other areas of fine-tuning will soon realize that fewer resources are available. It seems that publishers don't sense as broad a market for the fine-tuning issues. Moreover, we quickly learn that if we're going to effect a change in behavior, we need to do more than assign books to be read or verses to be memorized. We have to be more creative than that.

What follows is a program of personal growth and discipleship that tries to take seriously these various concerns. But first a disclaimer: There's always a risk in prescribing a specific program because there's no such thing as "one-size-fits-all" programming. Perhaps it would be better to think of this program idea as a template, an attempt to address the need for leaders to communicate at a deeper level with their students. It will be left up to those who read these words to adapt the idea to their respective ministry contexts.

Onward Bound: A Program Idea for the Contribute Level

Based on Paul's words in Philippians 3:12-14, *Onward Bound* is a program that stresses the ongoing process of spiritual growth and long-term passionate pursuit. It was designed to be open to any students—middle school or high school—who are interested in a growth plan that would be personally tailored to meet their needs. The students should be told up front that this will be time-consuming and that they're expected to make and keep a 13-week commitment to the program. From this description, it's pretty clear this would be a Disciple Level or Develop Level program (see chapter 5); it's designed for students who are willing to take the initiative for their own spiritual growth. There should be some publicity with the initial launch of the program (see promo piece below), and then each student who signs up will be engaged individually through a three-phase strategy.

ONWARD BOUND
A PROGRAM OF PERSONAL GROWTH AND DISCIPLESHIP

If you are a person committed to Jesus Christ ... committed to growth ... committed to being stretched by God's Word and God's Spirit ... open to "pressing on" in your walk with Christ, *then, ONWARD BOUND is for you!*

> "I do not claim that I have already become perfect. I press on for the prize of the upward call of God in Christ Jesus. Of course, my brothers, I really do not think that I have made it; the one thing I do, however, is to forget what is behind me and do my best to reach what is ahead."
>
> —Paul (Philippians 3:12-14)

What is Onward Bound?—Onward Bound is a totally new program for the UMYF, but the concept is as old as Christianity. Onward Bound is a program designed to meet the needs of the many in our fellowship who are eager and ready to chart a course of personal Christian growth for themselves, that will help them to focus specifically on some areas in which they personally need to grow.

Who can take part in the Onward Bound program?—The Onward Bound program is open to every member of our UMYF Fellowship, but that doesn't mean everybody should do it. There are some in our group who, in addition to the regular Bible studies, etc., we have each week at Cornerstone and Sunday School, desire to get some individual encouragement and guidance for areas that they really want to zero in on. It will require commitment, and some time to meet with your growth partner at least once every week or two.

How does it work?—Onward Bound consists of two phases: (1) Evaluation: Finding some areas in which you feel you need to grow; helping each person discover some areas that need work which the person might not even be aware of; spending some time considering your strengths and weaknesses. (2) Focus: Choosing an area to really focus in on; discussing this area with Duffy and your growth partner and determining a growth strategy that will involve Scripture memorization, sharing what you've learned with others, reading some material that may help you work on the area you've chosen, and then putting what you've learned into practice.

How do I join?—Just sign your name on the form below, and then make an interview appointment with Duffy *immediately*.

ONWARD BOUND:_____ Phone:_____

Phase 1: Evaluation

The first step is to help each student explore and consider areas in which he or she needs to grow. This could be done by using three sources of input:

Personal Interviews: The Student's Input. Begin with the students. They signed up for this—presumably, each of them is hoping to work on something. This needs to be the starting place, and my experience is that most students benefit from having someone help them define some growth goals. Someone can realize, for example, that she needs a personal trainer, but that doesn't mean she'll know which exercises will be most helpful. Here are some questions to spark this conversation:

- Which is the toughest place for you to live out your faith, and why? Your family, school, friendships, boyfriend/girlfriend, church?
- How would you complete the following statement: *I think I could be more faithful to Jesus if I could...*
- What's the hardest part about being a disciple of Jesus?

You might also invite students to take some variation of the self-examination test that John Wesley prepared for his own account-ability group.[6] (These questions probably should be adapted for a specific youth ministry context.)

1. Am I consciously or unconsciously creating the impression that I am better than I really am? In other words, am I a hypocrite?
2. Do I confidentially pass on to others what has been said to me in confidence?
3. Can I be trusted?
4. Am I a slave to dress, friends, work, or habits?
5. Am I self-conscious, self-pitying, or self-justifying?
6. Did the Bible live in me today?
7. Do I give the Bible time to speak to me every day?
8. Am I enjoying prayer?
9. When did I last speak to someone else about my faith?
10. Do I pray about the money I spend?

11. Do I get to bed on time and get up on time? (Habits of healthy living)
12. Do I disobey God in anything?
13. Do I insist upon doing something about which my conscience is uneasy?
14. Am I defeated in any part of my life?
15. Am I jealous, impure, critical, irritable, touchy, or distrustful?
16. How do I spend my spare time?
17. Am I proud?
18. Do I thank God that I am not as other people, especially as the Pharisees who despised the publican?
19. Is there anyone whom I fear, dislike, disown, criticize, hold a resentment toward, or disregard? If so, what am I doing about it?
20. Do I grumble or complain constantly?
21. Is Christ real to me?"

Parental Evaluation Forms. Parents of each student should be sent a short letter, signed by both you and their child, asking for honest input about various elements of their teenager's personal habits (use of free time, computer usage, accepting responsibility around the house, keeping his or her room acceptable, contributing to unity and health of the family, etc.). Make it clear in the letter that this parental input *will* be shared with the student. Not only does this invite parents to own the process of their teenager's spiritual growth, but it's also a great way to let parents know that you value their input and their role in the spiritual life of their teen.

Personal Interview: The Youth Leader's Input. The youth leader should meet privately and individually with each student to talk about some possible growth areas. These conversations could vary widely. It's possible the input might range from:

- "I'm wondering if there's a way we can help you improve the situation between you and your dad."
- "Have you thought about how your commitment to Jesus affects your approach to your school work?"
- "You have some leadership gifts that we need to develop."

- "Look, you've shared in small group about how you're struggling with pornography. Do you want me to help you work on that?"
- "What if you thought about soccer as not just a game you play, but an avenue for you to do ministry? What would that look like?"
- "I know you've been struggling with reading the Bible. I'd like to help you develop a deeper and more consistent devotional life."

The end product of this Evaluation Phase is to help the student articulate one or (at most) two Growth Goals. Don't try to tackle every issue in the first 13 weeks. It's better to make some headway with one or two Growth Goals than to identify 10 issues that you won't have time to address. After you've identified one or two Growth Goals, the student commits to a Growth Covenant based on these goals.

Phase 2: Growth Covenant
Drawing on the above information, a personally tailored program of growth will be created for each student. (See the example on the next page.) This Growth Covenant involves at least four categories of focus:

GROWTH COVENANT

"I do not claim that I have already become perfect. I press on for the prize of the upward call of God in Christ Jesus. Of course, my brothers, I really do not think that I have made it; the one thing I do, however, is to forget what is behind me and do my best to reach what is ahead."

—Paul (Philippians 3:12-14)

DATE_____

Please complete this growth covenant carefully, prayerfully, and completely. A covenant is like a promise, that to the best of your ability, with God's help, you will complete the assignments below. It's a promise to yourself, to God, and to your Growth Partner. This covenant is based on areas of growth that you've identified for special effort. Be willing to push yourself. Your Growth Partner is taking valuable time to meet with you. Make those meetings count. Try to meet with him/her a minimum of three to four times over the thirteen weeks - once every other week, if possible.

MY COVENANT: I,_____, in an effort to "press on for the prize of the upward call of God in Christ Jesus," do solemnly commit myself, with God's help, to grow in the following areas of my life. This is *not* my effort to get Jesus to love me more; it's my effort to be more fully open to what Christ has done *for* me and to what Christ's love can do *in* me. I understand that I will be held accountable for these goals and that my covenant to grow in these areas is not to be taken lightly.

REMEMBER: BE SPECIFIC!!

Goal One:_____

Goal Two:_____

It is **my responsibility** to meet with my growth partner. I will be responsible for setting up meetings on the following days/times:

No. 1_____ No. 2_____ No. 3_____ No. 4_____ No. 5_____ No. 6_____

This covenant is to be finished by_____(Date). In order to make progress toward these goals I have stated, I will work in the following growth areas with the assignments listed below:

SCRIPTURE:_____

READING:_____

PRACTICE:_____

SHARING:_____

Scripture. Each covenant should entail some element of Bible study or memorization—or both.

Other Reading. Students will be assigned to read a book or articles that give some insight into the area with which they struggle. This not only helps them to pursue their Growth Goals, but also teaches them to read Christian books—a great asset for long-term growth.

Practice. Each student will be given an assignment that involves actually putting one's Growth Goals into some observable behavior. For example, Steve's Covenant includes an agreement that he will keep a *life-log* of any arguments he has with his parents during the next two weeks, listing the time, circumstances, subject, and outcome of each disagreement. Then, Steve and his Growth Partner (see Phase Three) can look at this and see if there are any patterns that might be addressed to bring improvement in his relationship with his parents.

Sharing. Each Covenant will identify some arena (such as a small group, ministry team, or covenant group) in which the student can share his or her goals with other brothers and sisters, and report on his or her progress in pursuing growth toward those goals. For example, a student might share at a small group meeting about one thing he learned from the book he agreed to read. Or maybe a student talks about some steps she's taking to make better use of her time and not spend so much time on the computer. The idea here is to begin to forge the pattern set out by the writer of Hebrews: "And let us consider how we may spur one another on toward love and good deeds, not giving up meeting together, as some are in the habit of doing, but encouraging one another—and all the more as you see the Day approaching" (Hebrews 10:24-25).

Phase 3: Accountability

During Phase Three, over the course of 13 weeks, each student will meet with one of the ministry team members at least once every other week. Those who assume this mentor role are called *Growth Partners.* Growth Partners can be adults in the congregation or volunteer adult leaders, but essentially they're responsible for seeing that each student is making progress in his or her Covenant and, more than that, for helping students reflect on what they're learning through their various assignments. In time, as you get some high school juniors and seniors in the Develop Level, you might be able to incorporate them as Growth Partners.[7] These meetings would typically last 60 to 90 minutes. And they are the absolute key to the effectiveness of this strategy.

What we want to offer students here is practical instruction that goes beyond the usual, vague, "Get out there and be a blessing" pep talk, and we want to couple that with loving accountability. We also want to bathe the entire process in huge doses of encouragement. The goal is to help students make real progress in some of the trouble areas that impede their spiritual growth, and offer our leaders a format that invites a deeper contribution into the life of a student.

As with any system, the results are only as good as the people monitoring the system. The Growth Partners are critical to the program; they can make or break the whole idea. To restate a principle from earlier in this book, *If we give people Develop Level responsibility for a student's spiritual growth when they haven't assumed Disciple Level responsibility for their own spiritual growth, it will sabotage the whole idea.* Growth Partners should be chosen carefully, and parents shouldn't be discounted from the process.[8] Parents are uniquely suited and biblically called to be Growth Partners for their children (Deuteronomy 6:7ff).

The more specific the Growth Goals chosen in Phase Two, the better. It's easy to say, "I want to be more of a blessing to my family," but accountability is almost impossible to achieve with a fuzzy goal like that. Use the same criteria for shaping Growth Goals that might be used for shaping any type of objectives: Students should be encouraged to create goals that are *measurable* (Can they tell if they've hit the target or missed it?), *reachable* (Is it possible to accomplish this goal—or at least see some forward progress—in just 13 weeks?), and *ownable* (It needs to be the student's goal, not what the student *thinks* the leader wants the goal to be).

A final caution is that spiritual growth doesn't come through programs; it comes through people. Onward Bound is simply a structure designed to meet a need. Some needs may call for this structure to be adapted—or for a completely different structure altogether. The key is to find some means of encouraging our students to grow progressively into the image of Christ, and to facilitate the involvement of parents and other caring adults in the process. Sally shouldn't be ignored until she has some serious moral failure or simply drifts away from her faith. Nor does she need to be nagged into reconversion so that *this* time she can really, really, *really* get serious about Jesus. Like most growing things, what Sally needs is nurture, care, pruning, and the right environment.

The ideas offered on the preceding pages are merely suggestions, programming ideas for implementing what is clearly *not* a suggestion, but a biblical mandate. That mandate is personal, relational, incarnational investment in the lives of others. How we do that will vary from group to group, from ministry context to ministry context. But a youth ministry that builds passionate disciples of Jesus will always have at its core a commitment to move beyond instruction to emphasize direction.

NOTES

1. *Jerry Maguire*, directed by Cameron Crowe, TriStar Pictures, 1996.

2. Kenda Creasy Dean, *Practicing Passion: Youth and the Quest for a Passionate Church* (Grand Rapids, MI: Zondervan, 2006), 243.

3. A great resource for asking nonthreatening questions is the series of books published by Zondervan/Youth Specialties: *Would You Rather...?* (Fields, 1996), *More Would You Rather...?* (Fields, 2004) *Have You Ever...?* (Christie, 1998), *Unfinished Sentences* (Christie, 2000), and *What If...?* (Christie, 1996). I suggest keeping a copy of one of these books in the church van, the Sunday school classroom, and in your den at home. It's easy to grab one, throw out a question, and get kids talking.

4. Cited in Dale Carnegie, *How to Win Friends and Influence People* (New York: Pocket Books, 1990), 111. Of course, this can all become very manipulative, so we need to test our hearts constantly for that. But this kind of thing used to be called "good manners" or "being friendly," and Paul's writing suggests that it's possible to have genuine concern for people even while being intent on preaching to them the Word (1 Thessalonians 2:8). Some would say, "That's loving kids with an agenda"; and depending on whose agenda is being pursued, that's a legitimate concern. But a simple reading of the Gospels demonstrates that Jesus also had an agenda: "The Son of Man came to seek and to save the lost" (Luke 19:10). Christ's agenda clearly wasn't just about making contacts. He was intent on making disciples, "to seek and to save the lost."

5. For some fun affirmation strategies, see Doug Fields and Duffy Robbins, *Memory Makers* (Grand Rapids, MI: Zondervan, 1996).

6. Howard Culbertson, Professor of Missions and World Evangelism, Southern Nazarene University, http://home.snu.edu/~HCULBERT/selfexam.htm. "The first list appeared about 1729 or 1730 in the preface to Wesley's second *Oxford Diary*. Similar questions appeared in his 1733 *A Collection of Forms of Prayer for Every Day in the Week*. As late as 1781, Wesley published a list of questions like this in the *Arminian Magazine*."

7. For some of my more mature high school students at the Develop Level, serving as a Growth Partner was actually a part of their own personal Growth Covenant.

8. For more information and guidance on recruitment and screening of volunteer leaders, see Duffy Robbins, *Youth Ministry Nuts and Bolts (Revised and Updated): Organizing, Leading, and Managing Your Youth Ministry* (Grand Rapids, MI: Zondervan, 2010), chapters 10 and 11.

CHAPTER 9
TOOLS AND NOT JUST TALK

When I taught my daughter to drive, I realized it wasn't enough to teach her how to operate the car and understand the rules of the road. If I wanted her to drive very far, then I was going to have to give her some instruction in basic maintenance—how to fix a flat, how to change the oil, and how to refuel. In short, I had to equip her with some simple tools of upkeep in order to prepare her for a long journey. In the same way, if we want to nurture in our students a passionate faith, then we must give them the tools they'll need to refuel spiritually and work through those times when their spiritual lives seem flat.

Down through the centuries, these tools have remained pretty much the same. Our brothers and sisters in Christ have utilized three basic ones: *Bible Reading*, *Prayer*, and *Meditation*. Over the last 10 years, youth ministry has been blessed with the production of numerous resources to help youth workers equip their students in maintaining a walk with God. (See the Bibliography for some of these titles.) So while we won't try to reinvent those wheels in this book, we *will* put a new spin on some of them and pump a little enthusiasm into our commitment to make use of them.

Let's look at them one at a time:

BIBLE READING

In the dance of faith, Scripture reading offers rhythm, tempo, guidance, and melody—and all of it under the direction of the conducting baton of the Holy Spirit. Nurturing in students a love for God's Word is essential for building passionate disciples. As Paul wrote, "All Scripture is God-breathed and is useful for teaching, rebuking, correcting and training in righteousness, so that the servant of God may be thoroughly equipped for every good work" (2 Timothy 3:16-17).

Unfortunately, the Bible is a perplexing book for most teenagers—outdated, overrated, and misunderstood.

Several years ago I wrote a regular column for a monthly magazine published for teenage guys. It was an advice column called (get ready for this) "Yo, Duffy!" and the idea was that our readers would send in questions, and I'd respond to them with brevity, wit, insight, depth, and theological integrity (of course). In truth, brevity was the only one we nailed consistently; my editor saw to that! Our other unmet expectations were based on the hope that guys would write a diversity of questions and that they'd ask us about topics we actually *wanted* to write about—questions like:

"How can I have a better quiet time?"

"What's the best way to use my tithe?"

"Where can I buy good commentaries?"

"How can I make my Facebook page more evangelistic?"

"What if my mom says my room is *too* clean, but I still feel like cleaning it?"

Unfortunately, those questions appeared in my inbox about as often as wit and insight appeared in my outbox. Since the magazine had an all-male readership, at least 75 percent of the questions were about women. (Surprise!) Occasionally, the editor would send me some of these "unusable" questions with a note: "We're probably not going to print this guy's question, but we thought you might want to answer him anyway." Those were usually the best questions and the most fun to answer. What follows is one of my favorites:

Yo, Duffy:

What is the point of Song of Solomon?! First of all, there's nothing about God. Second of all, there's everything about lust, breasts, and sex. For example, 7:7-8. To me, the meaning of this is very clear; straddle a woman and grab her breasts. Or 8:10, which basically states: I have big breasts—therefore, my lover is happy.

If there is a spiritual meaning to all this, tell me! I need to know.

Doug, Lake Forest, CA[1]

I won't give you my entire response to this guy, but here's a portion of my letter:

> *Dear Doug:*
>
> *First of all, let me just say I appreciate your honesty. It's really refreshing! Secondly, I also think you have a remarkable gift for paraphrase. Thanks to your letter, my wife and I have decided to go back and study this book together!*

What struck me the most about Doug's letter (beyond his vivid prose) was that this was ultimately a question about hermeneutics. Here's a guy who was trying to understand the Bible. He was willing to read it, but he was struggling to make sense of it. That's significant for those of us who want to build teenage disciples. Guys like Doug don't need someone to charge them to read the Bible *more*; they need someone to help them read the Bible *better*.

For teenagers, reading the Bible quite often feels like trying to eat steak through a straw or enjoy soup with a steak knife. They've heard that it's supposed to be this wonderful meal, that it offers strength and sustenance, and that people really find it satisfying—but somehow they don't know how to take it in. And instead of leaving the Word nourished and filled, they leave the table hungry and discouraged.

That's why it's so important that we equip our students with the basic skills of inductive Bible study—called *inductive* because it's an approach that starts *in* the text and *in*vites the text to stimulate our thinking. If you already have a pretty good sense of inductive methodology, feel free to skip this next section. But for those who'd appreciate a simple overview, read on.

A Three-Step Guide to Inductive Bible Study

Obviously, there's a lot more to reading the Bible than just three easy steps. And no one is suggesting that just going through the motions of following this guide will usher a teenager into the throne room of God. But before you can run, you have to walk—and using this simple plan just might help your students read and better understand God's Word. It will build their personal Bible study around the three steps of *Observation*, *Interpretation*, and *Application*.

Step 1: Observation. The first step in Bible study is simply reading and observing what the text says. For example, if a student is reading one of the Gospel narratives (stories), she's going to ask: Who are the main characters? Where is the action taking place? What is the main thrust of the story? On the other hand, if it's a passage from Paul's letter to the Romans, it's not really a story; it's more instruction. In that case, the questions would focus more on the main topic. What is being taught here? Is this an explanation or a promise or a warning or a specific set of instructions? As students begin to desire a more in-depth study of Scripture, they may want to use some of the free online resources designed to help folks dig more deeply into the cultural, geographical, and historical details that make a passage come to life.[2]

This Observation step may require reading the passage through two or three times, both carefully and prayerfully. Remember, for example, that the Gospel writers were giving us more of a sketch than a full picture. (See John 21:25.) So although we don't want to read something *into* the lines of Scripture, we shouldn't be afraid to read *between them*. When we move through the Observation stage too quickly, we're apt to miss part of the picture God is trying to paint for us.

"For God so loved the world that he gave his only son so that who ever believed in him would not perish but have everlasting life."

See what I mean?

So, for example, if a student is dealing with Luke 19:1-10 (the Zacchaeus narrative), his reflection might begin with a reading of the text, perhaps two or three times, and then writing down on a sheet of paper everything he can observe about the story. Maybe he'd read it one time from the perspective of Luke (the narrator), but then a second time through the eyes of the townspeople, or from the standpoint of Zacchaeus. That's careful Observation—it's allowing the Light of God's Spirit to shine through the prism of his Word and then watching for the varied colors and reflections of Truth.

Step 2: Interpretation. Once your students have observed what the passage says, they're ready to think about what it means. That's the second step: Interpretation. From his Observation in Luke 19, a student might ask: What does Jesus mean by "the Son of Man came to seek and to save the lost"? Who is the "Son of Man," and why is he called that? Was Zacchaeus really "lost"? In what sense was Zacchaeus "lost"? Was he looking for hardwoods and ended up in a sycamore tree?

At this point the reader may begin asking questions about what the passage teaches: Is there a word for me here today? If it's a promise, to whom is it being made? Are there any conditions? If it's a warning, who's being warned? Why? What would this truth look like in today's world? Sometimes, it's even good for students to rewrite the passage in their own words. That may help them think through what the text is actually saying.

There are some very useful tools that will allow your students to dig more deeply into the text. Online version of these can be found at the websites listed in the Endnotes. These tools include:

- *Concordance.* A concordance lists all the words in the Bible and each verse in which that word is used. For example, if the "Yo, Duffy!" letter-writer, Doug, wanted to find out where the word *straddle* appears in the Bible, he could look up *straddle* in a concordance and it would give him the references of any verses that use that word.
- *Commentary.* A commentary records how Bible scholars through the centuries have done their own work of Observation, Interpretation, and Application on a given passage.
- *Bible Dictionary.* It's just what it sounds like. If your kids don't know a Hittite from a Jedi knight, or an Israelite from a Bud Light, the Bible dictionary simply explains what these biblical words mean.

Step 3: Application. The third step in inductive Bible study involves moving beyond the question of "What does it mean?" and asking, "What does it mean *for me*?" How should I apply what God is teaching here? How would this truth look in my life if I put it into practice? This is where Bible study becomes a little less comfortable. We're actually expected to live this stuff out. In the words of James, "Do not merely listen to the word, and so deceive yourselves. Do what it says" (James 1:22). If Bible study is a three-step dance, then this is usually where our toes get stepped on...or where some of us sliiiide!

Application is where we begin asking the "me" questions and the "we" questions. For example, going back to the Luke 19 passage, one might apply this passage by asking oneself:

- Have I been hiding from Jesus?
- How do I hide? Why?
- What keeps me up in the tree?
- Would I be willing to "come down at once" and welcome Jesus into my life? Into *all* parts of my life?
- Am I ever like those townspeople—judging and sneering from a distance because "there's no way God could love somebody as sinful and lame as so-and-so"? Are my friends?

One final word of encouragement here: The bottom line in Bible study is not just getting to know the Word of God; it's getting to know the God of the Word. Which method you teach your students isn't all that important. Remember The Ballroom Dancing Principle: It's not about the steps; it's about developing a relationship with our Partner. Don't be discouraged if your initial efforts are stiff and awkward. Effective Bible study is a skill one learns and develops with practice.

Other Ideas for Helping Students Explore the Word

While there are literally hundreds of teaching strategies for youth workers and pastors seeking to get students into the Word, there are few strategies that help students study the Word for themselves. And yet few tools are more essential for long-term travel on the way of faith.

Up until the mid-fifteenth century, every Bible in existence was written by hand—and not just written out, but often turned into gorgeous works of art.[3] Beyond some very serious hand cramps, imagine how amazing it must have been for scribes to write down all the words of Scripture, one by one, with their own hands. In our own keyboard culture, where educators have essentially opted to eliminate cursive handwriting from the curriculum, one of the more meaningful and practical ways we can get students into the text of Scripture is by encouraging them to write it out. Maybe it's best described as *holy plagiarism*. It's taking Scripture, word for word, and inviting students to write it out for themselves. We all have different learning styles, and for some people the simple act of writing—whether it's taking notes in class or copying down the words of Scripture—is a helpful way to experience the message and make it personal.

In fact, God had this instruction for the Old Testament kings:

When he takes the throne of his kingdom, he is to write for himself on a scroll a copy of this law, taken from that of the Levitical priests. It is to be with him, and he is to read it all the days of his life so that he may learn to revere the LORD his God and follow carefully all the words of this law and these decrees. (Deuteronomy 17:18-19)

The kings didn't really need to make another copy of the law. The Levites had one in their possession, and it would have been readily available to members of the royal family. But God wanted the king to write it down for himself—*with his own hand.*

Any of our students can do this—write out for themselves the words of God. It's simple, practical, and inexpensive to do. All it requires is blank paper and a pencil, or a brand-new journal and a really cool pen (or a youth room wall and a can of paint!).

Here are a few specific ideas:[4]

Journaling Scripture

Give students a journal and encourage them, over the course of a few weeks or months, to copy a chapter or even an entire book of the Bible—in small chunks, of course. The only "rule" is that they copy the text word for word. But as they're copying the text, you can invite them to make other changes as they wish. For example:

- They can turn sentences into lists.

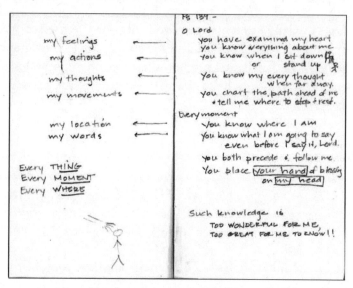

Figure 9-1 Bible Journaling: Turn Sentences into Lists

- They can underline, use all caps, or draw pictures for important words.

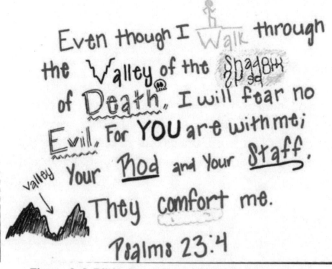

Figure 9-2 Bible Journaling: Highlight Key Words

• They can use different colored pens.

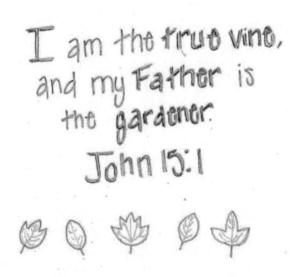

Figure 9-3 Bible Journaling: Different Colored Pens

• They can decorate the margins with artwork or doodling.

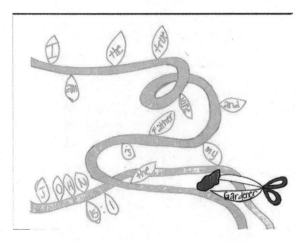

Figure 9-4 Bible Journaling: Doodles or Drawings to Illustrate the Text

• They can journal their thoughts, responses, and observations on the facing page or in between the lines.

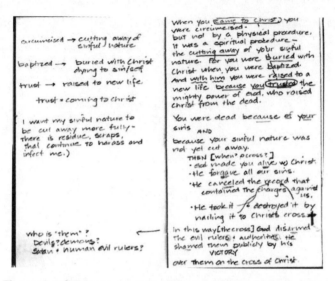

Figure 9-5 Bible Journaling: Commentary and Study Notes

Some students' copies might be really artsy and creative (Figure 9-6), and others may choose to play it straight. It doesn't matter. The key here is that they write out the words of Scripture for themselves.

Figure 9-6 Bible Journaling: More Elaborate and Artistic

Group Journaling

Students can also work together to create their own artistic presentation of a portion of Scripture. Let each student be responsible for a chapter, a section, or even just a single verse, then invite them to copy or decorate it any way they choose. Then, when you compile all of the students' completed sections, you can make copies of the finished text for everyone in the group. It makes a pretty cool artistic manuscript, showing each students' distinct contribution, and it would probably be something meaningful for the kids involved.

If you have small groups in your ministry, assign different sections of biblical text to each small group, and then compile them into a larger manuscript.

Bible on the Wall

Invite students to adopt a wall in your meeting space and decorate it with a Bible text. It can be done in a graffiti style or as some adaptation of the designs we've mentioned in previous sections. The wall could be divided so that small groups will decorate different parts of the wall, or it could be one big splashy wall text. It might…um…be a really good idea to get permission before you embrace this idea too heartily—especially if you're meeting in someone's home.

Figure 9-7 Bible on the Wall

If your meeting room includes a chalkboard, students can use colored chalk to highlight a focus passage for the day or emphasize a monthly theme. Some hardware or home-improvement stores even sell a "chalkboard" paint that would allow you to turn a bland wall into an ever-changing tapestry of artistic chalk drawings of Bible texts.

The Social Network Bible

Facebook and other social networking sites have a "verse of the day" option that you can utilize with your students. Organize Facebook groups where, instead of just choosing the "verse of the day" application, students would actually type out Scripture and post it or send it to one another.

The Old-School Social Network Bible

Remember chain letters? Well, first you have to remember *letters*— those archaic handwritten documents we once used to communicate with each other before emoticons were invented. Encourage your students to start a chain-letter copy of a particular Scripture passage, with each person writing out the next verse of the text in his or her own style, and then mailing it to the next member of the group. (Offer to show them how to seal an envelope and affix a stamp.)

Wordles

The website www.wordle.net allows visitors to paste text into a box, and then the site creates a unique design based on those words (for free!). So a student could type a Scripture passage into the program, and the software would create for them a *Wordle* based on that text. Here's one example:

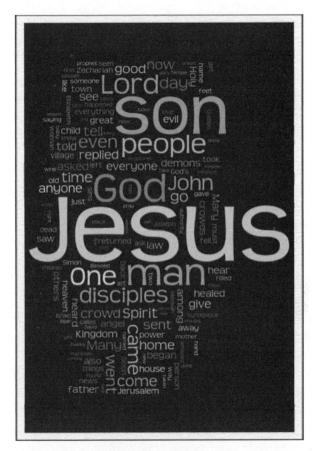

Figure 9-8 Wordles

The best part about inviting students to write out Scripture is that anybody can do it. It doesn't require any special ability, or faith, or even maturity. But it puts students' eyes directly on a portion of Scripture for a concentrated period of time. That can't be a bad thing. And if we truly believe that God's Word can transform human hearts and penetrate to where bone and spirit meet (Hebrews 4:12), then it *can* be a *very good* thing!

PRAYER

Helping growing Christians develop habits of prayer is a bit like teaching a child to talk. Children instinctively have the ability and the desire to cry out, to make themselves known; but it takes some practice before they learn how to clearly express what they're feeling. Similarly, most teenagers lack a lexicon for prayer. They hunger for God; they may not be aware of what to name this longing, but they feel it keenly and deeply. And when they do think about prayerful communication with God, it's usually in the terms and vocabulary of the culture—some combination of religious mush and cosmic room service.

One way we can help our students deepen their intimacy with Christ is by training them in the discourse, or the language, of prayer—helping them develop habits of communication with God. Just providing them with some elementary prayer strategies can help students develop confidence and feel at home even in the presence of God.

Let's look at a few of them:

One-Word Prayers

These are prayers limited to a single word or phrase. With this form of prayer, students can be prompted with instructions: "Let's think of one way we've seen God's love in our lives this week," or "Let's lay before God's throne one area of life that's holding us down this week."

Or students can be given these instructions: "I know some of you don't feel totally comfortable praying in our group. So rather than feel like you've got to pray some long prayer in front of everybody, I want you to think of a prayer request that you have tonight. Then think of one key word that lies at the heart of your request. As we spend the next few moments in prayer, I invite you to pray just that one-word prayer aloud, knowing that God will understand what's on your heart." So, for example, the prayer time might simply consist of students speaking words like *Help…Thanks…Dad…Come…Test… Forgive…Confusion…Gratitude.*

Hot-Seat Prayers

With this simple idea, you'll invite one student to sit in the middle of the circle while the rest of the group offers a prayer of support, affirmation, or intercession.[5]

Open-Ended Prayers

The leader begins the prayer time with a phrase that students may complete out loud. For example, the leader might begin by saying something like, "Lord, I thank you for...," and then individual students could take turns finishing the sentence as their own prayer: "...my friends," "...my mom's new job," "...helping me work through the stuff I've been asking you about," or "...your Son, Jesus."

Or the leader might say, "Lord, I ask you for strength this week as I...," and the students might respond with: "...struggle with resentment," "...work on my final paper for English," "...talk to Chad about Jesus," or "...try to understand what Mom and Dad are going through."

Build a Prayer

Students stand together in a circle and, one at a time, pray aloud around the circle. One student begins a sentence, the next student completes it, a third student either adds more to that first sentence or begins a new one, and so on. For example,

> Student 1: Lord, I pray that we might...
> Student 2: ...be thankful for all you have given to us, such as...
> Student 3: ...Uhh, our friends, and our parents, and...
> Student 4: ...Aunts and uncles and...
> Student 5: ...Grandparents and neighbors...

You get the idea.

Responsive Prayer

This strategy is part liturgy and part prayer, as students will repeat, in unison, a phrase or refrain in response to the leader's prayer. For example:

> LEADER: For our selfishness with friends—always wanting to have it our own way...
> STUDENTS: We ask, Lord, for your forgiveness.
> LEADER: For our blindness to others' needs, when ours seem so important and obvious...
> STUDENTS: We ask, Lord, for your forgiveness.

Popcorn Prayers

Kids stand up randomly and pray a one-word or one-sentence prayer.

Written Prayers

Students are given time to write out a prayer that can be read aloud by the leader or the students themselves. If they're not sure how to do this, tell them to think of it like writing a letter to God. Or for a more familiar structure, tell them to put their prayer in the form of a tweet (140 characters) or text.

Altar Prayers

Using the chancel area of a church sanctuary, spend some extended time praying around the altar.

Prayer Calendar

Print out a prayer calendar for your students so they'll have a specific prayer focus for any given day in a month. Here are two examples:[6]

May	Dear friend, I pray that you may enjoy good health and that all may go well with you, even as your soul is getting along well (3 John 2).					
Sun	**Mon**	**Tue**	**Wed**	**Thu**	**Fri**	**Sat**
	1 G. Jefferson	2 M. Manson	3 P. Jacobson	4 R. Jones	5 S. Somers	6 J. Eastman
7 R.	8 B. Clinton	9 S. Smith	10 L. Powers	11 R.	12 O. Grav	13 A. Adam
14 M.	15 T.	16 W.	17 T. Crockett	18 B. Graham	19 M. Kramer	20 D. Nowell
21 F. Parks	22 M. Jagger	23 D. Bennett	24 P. Cochran	25 B. Soears	26 K. Wright	27 S.
28 J. Seinfeld	29 L. Greene	30 E. Goodfield	31 M. Mouse			

We can pray for each other:
that we grow deeper in our love for Jesus
that we are bold in our witness for Christ
that we stand strong in temptation
that God allows us to do our best in school.

2015

August

SUN	MON	TUE	WED	THU	FRI	SAT
	People in Rwanda **1**	1st Pres. Pardeeville **2**	A Friend who doesn't Know Christ **3**	Andrew Jed in New York **4**	People who are hungry **5**	Lisa + Scott **6**
The Gaza Strip **7**	That you might understand God's Power **8**	Your Advisor **9**	People on Vacation **10**	Freshmen **11**	People with AIDS **12**	Homeless Meal **13**
Junior High Group **14**	Backpack Trip **15**	People who live on Telegraph **16**	Senior High Group **17**	Family **18**	Juniors **19**	Senior Citizens **20**
Church Choir **21**	Students going to College **22**	Sophomores **23**	Kids in Mexico **24**	College Department **25**	Oak and Pen'al Mission **26**	Current Administration **27**
See You at the Pole **28**	Seniors **29**	People in Prison **30**	Neil Jung (new intern) **31**			

Objects of Prayer

Place five to ten small items at the front of the room as prayer prompts. Choose items that connect with the everyday lives and concerns of your students, as well as the world around them. For example, the objects might include a set of keys, some hiking boots, a rock, a cup, a cell phone, a bandage, a ball, a bike helmet, and a ring. You might choose to have these items illuminated only by the light of a candle. Then, invite students to use one of those objects as a prayer prompt. They could pray silently or aloud. Students would build off one of those objects to offer a prayer of petition, or a prayer of praise, or a prayer of thanksgiving.[7]

ACTS Prayers

Divide the prayer time into four two-minute segments using the acrostic A.C.T.S. Lead the students (or invite four different students to lead their peers) in an eight-minute session of prayer, allowing two minutes each for:

A (Adoration): Praising God for who he is

C (Confession): Confessing to God our sins (where we've fallen short)

T (Thanksgiving): Thanking God for what he does
S (Supplication): Asking God to supply our needs
    ("supply-cation")

You may want to signal the end of each two-minute segment with the sound of a quiet bell that indicates movement from one type of prayer to the next.

Diamond Prayers

Diamond Prayers allow each student to create a personalized written prayer in response to a series of specific prompts. The words of the completed prayer form the shape of a diamond. (See below for a blank copy of the form and a sample of a completed prayer.) Invite each student to prayerfully fill out the blanks in his or her diamond. Then invite some willing students to read their Diamond Prayers out loud. Obviously, the prayer as it's currently constructed would require some vulnerability among participants. If you don't think your group is there yet, change the various prompts to fit your situation or to flow out of a specific truth you've taught.

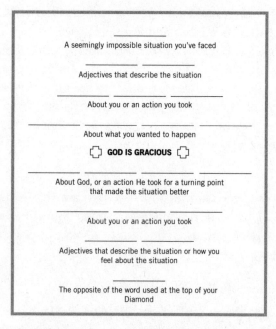

_____
A seemingly impossible situation you've faced

_____   _____
Adjectives that describe the situation

_____   _____
About you or an action you took

_____   _____
About what you wanted to happen

⊕ **GOD IS GRACIOUS** ⊕

_____   _____   _____   _____
About God, or an action He took for a turning point
that made the situation better

_____   _____   _____
About you or an action you took

_____   _____
Adjectives that describe the situation or how you
feel about the situation

_____
The opposite of the word used at the top of your
Diamond

Figure 9-11 Diamond Prayer (blank)

Figure 9-12 Diamond Prayer (completed)

MEDITATION

Meditation is one of those words that makes some Christians suspicious and virtually all teenagers nervous. We're not sure what to do with it. Is it some sort of mystical alchemy? Is it prayer or casting spells? Is it eastern religion or something out of Harry Potter? When teens hear *meditation*, most think of something weird and esoteric like going into a closet, turning off all the lights, listening to some music by the Sun Ra Arkestra, reading a passage from Oprah, and smoking oatmeal.

On the contrary, meditation is a very biblical concept. God's Word tells us: "Keep this Book of the Law always on your lips; meditate on it day and night, so that you may be careful to do everything written in it" (Joshua 1:8).

But students need the right tools to help them focus their minds on God's truth. Biblical meditation isn't sending students out into the woods and telling them to "Think deeply about stuff until I call you back." Biblical meditation is about an encounter made possible when two conditions are taken seriously: (1) There's a God who's willing to speak; and (2) There's a heart that's willing to hear. Because teenagers live in a world of noise and distraction, these two conditions seldom happen by accident. Wise youth workers who want to build lasting faith will intentionally create for their students such times and places.

Typically, that will mean being attentive to both ambiance and circumstance. We'll want to set the proper atmosphere (with special attention to quiet, focus, lighting, and room arrangement, plus sensitivity to the commitment level of the students, etc.) and offer our students some avenues of encounter.

Here are some possible strategies:

Directed Meditation

You can use passages from books, magazine articles, or Scripture as a way of offering students a few seed thoughts to chew on. Caution: If it's a written piece, be aware of the length. Although this guideline could flex, depending on the commitment level of the students involved, varying reading abilities and short attention spans suggest that it probably shouldn't take more than 10 minutes to read an article for directed meditation.

Beyond that qualification, the only other factor in choosing a reading of some kind would be that it's not so much educational as it is *realizational*. In other words, the point of reading the article is not so much to fill students' heads with new information as it is to help them perhaps realize some new truth about themselves and their relationship with God.

Here's one example, based on Luke's account of Jesus' healing of a crippled woman:[8]

Read:

Luke 13:11-13

And a woman was there who had been crippled by a spirit for eighteen years. She was bent over and could not straighten up at all. When Jesus saw her, he called her forward and said to her, "Woman, you are set free from your infirmity." Then he put his hands on her, and immediately she straightened up and praised God.

Reflect:

What if *you* were the woman "crippled by a spirit for eighteen years"? For the last eighteen years of your life, your entire horizon ended about a yard in front of your feet; your experience of a sunset doesn't involve splashing colors, but growing shadows. Your relationships are marked not by smiles and eye contact, but by the sound of a voice and the sight of familiar feet. What would it be like to spend all day, every day, staring at the ground? What if you could never look up?

In the space below, jot down some of the ways your life would be different if you spent the next 24 hours "bent over." Maybe it would be a sight you wouldn't see—a friend's smile, the sunset, your computer screen. Relationships you couldn't enjoy fully. Activities you couldn't possibly do.

If you were unable to straighten up at all, how would your life be "crippled"? Close your eyes for a few moments to imagine what that might be like. Then jot down your responses below.

After some time of quiet, invite the students to come back and share their experiences.

Path-Finding

This takes a little preparation work, but it's another interesting way of helping students do the kind of reflection that's so often steamrolled by a culture of rush and busy-ness. Begin by brainstorming about specific locations that are within walking distance of your meeting place. Needless to say, you'll want to be prudent with regard to safety and traffic concerns, and you may need to adapt these suggestions depending on the age and commitment level of your students. The idea is to develop a path of meditation that will direct students to various locations around the vicinity of your meeting site. And then at each location, students will be given thought-provoking reflection questions that connect with the particular station. For example:

Station 1—A Bank: "What are you banking on in your life? What is your security?"

Station 2—A Cemetery: "All the people buried here had dreams, hopes, and plans just like you do. Now that their lives are over, many of them have left behind a legacy of families and friends, lives in which they've invested themselves. But for others, including some who made important decisions and lots of money, all they've left behind is what stands on top of their grave. When your life is over, what do you hope to leave behind?"

Station 3—A Construction Site: "What are you 'building' with your life? What will this 'building' accomplish? Will it be a monument to yourself? Will it be a monument to God? Will it be a place of recreation? Worship? Are you 'building' something that will outlive you?"

Station 4—Service Station: "What is the 'fuel' in your life? What kinds of things motivate you and get you moving?"

Students should bring along a notepad and something to write with; encourage them to jot down their thoughts at each site. Then, when everyone gathers back at your usual meeting space, students should be invited to share some of their insights.

Personal Parable

Jesus was a master at using parables as a way of prompting deeper reflection. These short, sometimes open-ended illustrations and object lessons provided windows through which his listeners could hear or see some spiritual truth in a new way. This "Personal Parables" activity will work well whether you're meeting in a church building or community center, camping out in the woods, or simply spending a day in a park. Give students about 20 minutes or less to go out and find some object that either describes their relationship with God, tells something about who they are, or illustrates some lesson they're learning about the Christian life. Tell them to go out alone and explain that this will be 20 minutes spent in silence.

The objects the students choose to bring back with them aren't all that important. I've seen students return with everything from an empty canteen, to a rock, to a trailside flower that had been stepped on. When students gather again, allow each to share his or her personal parable—the story of why that particular item was chosen.

This meditation exercise has three goals: (1) We want to develop in students a pattern of watching for God in their lives; (2) We want to help them listen for God in the midst of their everyday walk; and (3) We want to give students their own vocabulary for talking about what God is doing in their lives.

Lectio Divina

The ancient practice of *lectio divina* is an avenue of encounter that combines all three of the dance steps—Bible reading, prayer, and meditation—into a seamless movement with God.[9] *Lectio divina* comes from two Latin words that literally mean "divine reading." At its heart is a very simple notion: *God wants to speak to us; but to hear him, we have to be willing to listen.*[10]

The problem is that our kids live in a loud world, and God often speaks in the quiet. The practice of *lectio divina* gives students a place in their lives to hear God. This spiritual discipline centers on *slowly* reading a short passage of Scripture a number of times, and in a way that allows the space and time for God to speak to the heart through that passage. With *lectio*, the emphasis is not on content, but on contemplation. It's a discipline that invites us to listen at a deeper level. Bible study is an activity, something you do—you read a chapter, you underline key verses and words, perhaps you make notes of your own insights and findings in the margins. It's important and it's helpful. But the main organ of hearing is the mind. *Lectio* begins with a word, a verse, a picture, a hint of God. Its goal is to move us from listening with the head to listening with the heart, from activity to receptivity. It's been described as a contemplative exercise in which "the mind meets the heart" so the heart can meet God.

Typically, *lectio divina* is practiced in four movements: *Lectio*, *Meditatio*, *Oratio*, and *Contemplatio*. At first, it sounds a little like the dessert menu at Bertucci's. But actually, these four words, these four stages, can help students develop a habit of clearing their minds and allowing God to excavate their hearts so he can take them to new depths in their relationship with him.

Stage 1: *Lectio.* The first step of *lectio* is reading the passage of Scripture—not reading to get through it, not even reading to get the facts, but reading to get focused. This is critical. Read slowly. Be unhurried. This is gentle listening. You don't fully appreciate all the facets of a diamond by driving by it in a car; and you won't fully appreciate a Bible text by cruising through each sentence on your way to the next paragraph. This is not drive-by devotions.

You want to encourage your students to read slowly.

Stage 2: *Meditatio.* We've already observed how the word *meditation* causes some people to get stuck. But biblically speaking, meditation has nothing to do with closing our eyes and trying to communicate with a rainbow. Instead, meditation is taking time to think about, to savor, and to deeply consider. For example, as the amazing events of that first Christmas unfolded around the Virgin Mary, we're told that she meditated on these happenings: "Mary treasured up all these things and *pondered them in her heart*" (Luke 2:19). Notice that phrase: *pondered them in her heart. Ponder* is a word that tells us something about what meditation is; *in her heart* is a phrase that tells us something about where it happens.

The Hebrew word for *meditation* suggests that it means "to chew slowly." In this second stage of *lectio divina*, we take time to chew and re-chew a passage of Scripture—rather than just reading it once and buzzing on to the next mouthful. I often describe it to teenagers as what happens when you're eating a peanut butter and jelly sandwich that has too much peanut butter on it. You're sitting there at the lunch table, and when you bite into that thing, it's like oral quicksand. You don't just swallow and move on to the bag of Fritos. You chew; and then you chew some more—you take your time with each bite. That's *meditatio.*

Stage 3: *Oratio.* Having read the text slowly and listened carefully, the next step in this dance of communion with God is *oratio*—talking to God in prayer. If the first two stages are where we allow God to talk to us, *oratio* is our response to God. It is conversation that informs us *and* shapes us. It describes the process of offering ourselves to God in obedience, the response of an open heart that hears the voice of God. First, we open ourselves to God with concentrated listening; then, we respond to God with consecrated obedience. It is this rhythm of conversation and consecration that is described as *oratio*, the third stage of *lectio divina*.

Stage 4: *Contemplatio.* The final stage of *lectio divina* is *contemplatio* or contemplation. It is simply resting in the presence of God. Imagine a small child nestled in the lap of her father, saying nothing, but completely content in the closeness of that moment—hearing his slow breathing, feeling the stubbles of his beard, and comforted by his steady arms and strong hands that cradle her head. Or imagine two friends sitting next to the campfire: They've already talked about that day's hike, adventures shared, vistas seen, wrong trails taken, where the journey has led them, and where it may lead them tomorrow. Now, they simply share the silence and stare into the flames together—quietly, contentedly. Like basking in the rays of warm sunshine, *contemplatio* is basking in the presence of the Father. It's a time of silence, allowing our intimacy with God to go beyond the place that words can take us.

In some ways, this final stage may be the most difficult part of the *lectio* exercise because it feels like we ought to be *doing* something. One Benedictine monk describes it in these terms:

> In contemplation we cease from interior spiritual *doing* and learn simply to *be*, that is to rest in the presence of our loving Father. Just as we constantly move back and forth in our exterior lives between speaking and listening, between questioning and reflecting, so in our spiritual lives we must learn to enjoy the refreshment of simply *being* in God's presence.[11]

Whenever you invite students into *lectio*, you'll want to use words like *linger, bask,* and *savor*. This is the language of intimacy, words that invite us to experience and enjoy the embrace of the Father.

TOOLS IN THE TOOLBOX

Are there other faith-building tools that haven't been mentioned above? Absolutely! Most notably—doing acts of mercy and living in community, to name just two. But the main point is that students need to be equipped with tools for the journey. A good push can get them going, but maintenance and refueling are the critical tools to keep them moving forward.

In chapter 10, we'll consider the power of memory.

NOTES

1. Actual name withheld.

2. For example, BibleGateway.com; Gospelcom.net; StudyLight.org; Biblestudytools. com.

3. To see a sample of one such ancient text from the Gospel of John, see http:// upload.wikimedia.org/wikipedia/commons/f/fa/Wycliffe_John_Gospel.jpg. For a modern, exquisite example of a hand-drawn pictorial text (the project began in 1998), see *The St. John's Bible* at http://www.saintjohnsbible.org/process/.

4. Thanks to Crystal Kirgiss, a good friend, a great communicator, and a creative teacher, for developing the material in this section. For more information about Crystal's books, see http://www.harpercollins.ca/authors/90001299/Crystal_Kirgiss/ index.aspx.

5. Obviously, this needs to be done with some sensitivity. The last thing you want is some student sitting in the middle of a prayer circle with no one offering a prayer of thanksgiving. It would be better to skip this idea than to risk a hurtful situation.

6. These calendars are based on templates included in the Youth Specialties *ArtSource* CD-ROM (Grand Rapids, MI: Zondervan, 1995). Other free prayer calendar templates are available online.

7. This idea comes from my dear friend Helen Musick, with whom I coauthored *Everyday Object Lessons for Youth Groups* (Grand Rapids, MI: Zondervan, 1999).

8. This meditation is taken from Maggie and Duffy Robbins, *Enjoy the Silence: A 30-Day Experiment in Listening to God* (Grand Rapids, MI: Zondervan, 2005), 65.

9. Some of this material is adapted from Maggie and Duffy Robbins' *Enjoy the Silence*. See that book for more suggestions using *lectio divina* with youth.

10. Check out Psalm 19:1-4; John 1:1, 14; Romans 1:18-21; and Romans 2:14-15 to learn more about God's desire to make himself known to us.

11. Fr. Luke Dysinger, O.S.B., *Accepting the Embrace of God: The Ancient Art of Lectio Divina.* A free PDF file of this document is available at http://www. valyermo.com/ld-art.html.

CHAPTER 10
MEMORIES AND NOT JUST MEETINGS

When I read through 2 Timothy 3:10-11, I imagine what it might be like in heaven someday to hear Paul and Silas, or Barnabas, or Luke, or Timothy recount old war stories—episodes of danger and difficulty, adventure and wonder, regaling listeners with how time and time again they witnessed the faithfulness of God. I've actually had glimpses of this in much smaller ways—sitting, for example, at a campfire and listening to youth group kids recount their memories of how they've seen God in the midst of work projects, backpacking trips, retreats, raucous laughter, and other incidents I won't recall in print. Reading Paul's words, we're led to believe that memories can be a powerful means of building faith:

> *You, however, know all about my teaching, my way of life, my purpose, faith, patience, love, endurance, persecutions, sufferings—what kinds of things happened to me in Antioch, Iconium and Lystra, the persecutions I endured. Yet the Lord rescued me from all of them.* (2 Timothy 3:10-11)

One of our most significant tasks as youth workers is to create memories for our kids. We need to think of ourselves not just as program directors, but also as *memory makers*. Memories are a gift we give to our students that cannot be taken away with time. Like those two disciples on the road to Emmaus, memories give our students a way of walking forward by looking backward and saying, "Were not our hearts burning within us?" (Luke 24:32).

Unfortunately, in a culture of overstimulation, where kids are numbed into oblivion, memories are hard to come by. I remember a parents' meeting where a mom asked our middle school pastor what he did with the kids on Tuesday night at Prime Time. She explained politely, "Every week, when I pick up my son and ask him what happened tonight at youth group, he says the same thing: 'Nothing.' I know he's been in a room at the church for 90 minutes, but I always worry a little about what he's taking out of the room when it's over." I wanted to step in for my colleague and remind this mom that "Nothing" is the stock answer that a teenager offers to virtually any question posed by an adult; she would have gotten the very same response had she asked, "Honey, what was that mushroom cloud that engulfed the middle school today?" But instead, I channeled my frustration into two questions:

1. What is it that makes something memorable?
2. Why is it that church is so often, and for so many, so utterly forgettable?

Before you read any further, take some time to respond to that first question by making a list of the factors that, in your own estimation, make a memory *memorable*.

Here's my list:[1]

- When it includes the element of *SURPRISE*
- When something is *OUTRAGEOUS* (meaning, literally, "that which is beyond the bounds of convention")
- When it allows us to *MAKE FRIENDS* or build community;
- When it's something we *EXPERIENCE* on a lot of different levels
- When it involves some *TRADITION* that lodges it in our minds
- When it's *HUMOROUS*—we usually remember moments of hearty laughter
- When there is an *INTENSITY* of experience—something really difficult or really pleasant
- When something is *NEW* to us (we usually remember that first time or that first taste or that first visit)
- When *GOD SHOWS UP* (Had someone asked those folks walking out of the Pentecost gathering in Acts 2, "What happened in there?" I don't think anybody would have answered, "Nothing.")

So how did your list turn out? Was there any overlap with the one above?

Now, let's do an experiment: Using either your own list or the one I've provided (it's already part of the table below), think back to the last five times you convened your students for a gathering—anything from Sunday school, to club, to a retreat, to a game night, to a worship service, to a work project. List those five events across the top of the chart below. Then go through the chart and, for each element of memory, put a check in the column if you think *your students* would say that characteristic was true of that particular ministry event.

Memory Factors	Example Sunday School	Gathering 1	Gathering 2	Gathering 3	Gathering 4	Gathering 5
Surprise						
Outrageous						
Make Friends/ Build Community	X					
Experience						
Tradition	X					
Humorous						
Intensity						
New						
God Shows Up						

As you look back over the completed table, you can get a pretty good sense of how, when, and why (or why not?) your program gives students the gift of faith-memories. What are we doing to give our students their own Iconiums, Lystras, and Antiochs—memories of love, suffering, and endurance that allow them to "observe our teaching, our way of life, our faith"? What it all boils down to is this simple takeaway: *The more we can build these factors into the various elements of our ministry, the more likely it is that they will be memorable.*

Let's look at some strategies for making memorable youth ministry.

Un-Testimony Service

At the end of a weekend retreat or a week of camp, most of us usually take the time to allow students to share about decisions they've made for Christ. That's great. But in addition to that, ask some willing students to give a word of "testimony" about why they *don't* feel they can make that commitment yet. This is a great time for you to affirm the sincere "seeker" in his or her search, and it also helps to promote honest questions and open ministry among group members.

Foot-Washing Ceremony

Following the Lord's example in John 13, students will wash one another's feet. There should be two or three small basins of water, along with two or three towels in the center of a circle of students (10 or fewer). Students will sit quietly in an attitude of prayer as each student gets up and washes the feet of one other person.

Instructions can designate that students are to wash the feet of a person whom they've come to know better, a person from whom they've felt real love, a person they really admire, a person they'd like to know better, or just a person whose feet are smelly and in need of a good washing.

You may want to have some quiet music playing in the background, or allow some quiet group singing.

Experiential Worship

Experiential worship is nothing more than an invitation for students to pay attention to God by using all five of their senses. It begins with a fundamental recognition that God speaks to us in different ways and that he is big enough and real enough to make himself known through more than just the senses of hearing and seeing that dominate most church services. Consider, for example, the experiential emphasis in a passage like Psalm 34:8—"Taste and see that the LORD is good." While such a sensory focus to worship may feel innovative to some of us, it's hardly new to Christendom. For centuries our brothers and sisters in more liturgical traditions have used aromas and movement and ritual to focus more vividly on the presence of God in their midst.

Rather than inventory the many resources for experiential worship that are already available, let's consider just one element of liturgy and how we could make it more real for our students. Here are some ideas for making the Eucharist a time of memorable communion:[2]

- Have students go with the pastor or priest to visit the sick in the hospital or shut-ins in their homes and help serve Communion.
- Let the students read the Scripture lesson or service of worship while Communion is being served.
- Meet at someone's home and have the students make the bread to be used on the Communion table.
- Show a video clip of the Last Supper from one of the "Jesus films" (*Jesus of Nazareth*, etc.) Take Communion as Jesus leads

the disciples through the breaking of the bread and the drinking of the cup.
- Use DaVinci's portrait of *The Last Supper*. Have the picture set up in the center of the room or displayed so everyone can see it. Ask: "Who are you most like in this picture? Which disciple best portrays where you'd be sitting?" Discuss the feelings and thoughts you have or the questions you'd want to ask Jesus if you'd been present that night.
- Using only mime, have some students who are gifted in drama act out the words of Christ at the Last Supper. Have the rest of the students take the elements in silence while they observe this dramatic interpretation of the event.
- Go to the home of one of your church members. Have a room set up with pillows on the floor and candlelight. As the students arrive and enter the room, set the scene for them: They've been invited to a great dinner party. However, the dinner party will be much different from what they expect. It will actually be Communion.
- Make wine or juice goblets out of pottery. Display them on the Communion table.
- As you take Communion, have each student play the role of a biblical character. The student will share his or her character's story before taking the elements. Each story will begin with the words, "I remember when Jesus...

> ...touched my eyes and I saw the sky for the first time" (John 9:1-12);
> ...healed my daughter" (Mark 5:22-43);
> ...told me everything I knew about myself" (John 4:5-29).

Pre-arranged "Disaster"
We all know that kids usually talk about the "bus breaking down" more than they talk about the retreat the bus was taking them to. What about staging a bus breakdown a mile from the camp and having kids hike the last mile? If your church bus is like most church vehicles, it runs so poorly that you can't even guarantee you'll make it to the pre-arranged "breakdown" point—but that just adds an additional element of mystery. As a variation on the same idea, plan

to have the bus "break down" in a rough part of town where you have (unbeknownst to the kids) already arranged to have the students housed for the night in a homeless shelter.

Pre-arranged "Disaster" 2
Plan for a "power outage" on the last night of camp, and suggest that "all of us spend the last night of camp here around the fire."

Surprise Hitchhiker
Plan a retreat around the theme of showing compassion toward others. And then, while you're traveling together to the retreat location, drive by a staged car breakdown (the uglier and scuzzier the car, the better). Stop to pick up the driver who is dirty, smelly, unshaven, and acting a little weird. When the first session begins later that night, allow the students to discover that this "stranger" was actually their retreat speaker. Talk about how the group responded to this stranger in their midst.

Planned Mischief
We all know that kids can't wait to sneak out and raid another cabin during camp. So set it up so that the guys in one cabin think they're going to sneak over to one of the women's cabins and surprise the girls with a water balloon attack. Then secretly prearrange with the counselor in the girls' cabin that when the guys stage their surprise attack at 2:00 a.m., she'll be sure that all the girls are out of the cabin, well-hidden among the nearby trees, and armed to the teeth with water balloons. When the guys bust into the cabin and discover nobody's home—then, out of the darkness, 10 girls will scream, "CHARGE!"

BETTER THAN "NOTHING"
Wise youth workers understand the faith-building power of memory. It's what led Moses to institute the Passover ritual, telling the elders of Israel, "Obey these instructions as a lasting ordinance for you and your descendants" (Exodus 12:24-27).

It was that faith-building power of memory that led Samuel to set up a stone between Mizpah and Shen, and name it Ebenezer, saying, "Thus far the LORD has helped us" (1 Samuel 7:12).

It was that faith-building power of memory that led Jesus at the Last Supper to take the bread, give thanks and break it, and give it to them, saying, "This is my body given for you; do this in *remembrance* of me" (Luke 22:19, emphasis added).

It was that faith-building power of memory that led Peter to write, "So I will always *remind* you of these things, even though you know them and are firmly established in the truth you now have. I think it is right to *refresh your memory* as long as I live in the tent of this body" (2 Peter 1:12-13, emphasis added).

It's the faith-building power of memory that helps us to move our students from "Nothing" to...

S URPRISE
O UTRAGEOUS
M AKE FRIENDS
E XPERIENCE
T RADITION
H UMOROUS
I NTENSITY
N EW
G OD SHOWS UP

NOTES

1. This material is adapted from a book I coauthored with Doug Fields, *Memory Makers* (Grand Rapids: MI, Zondervan, 1996).

2. Helen Musick and I composed this list for a Youth Specialties CORE seminar we led together in 2004. As was usually the case when we worked together, the best ideas were hers.

CHAPTER 11

AUTHENTIC PASSION

We began the second section of this book with a story about a photograph, an elderly man, and a poignant conversation at a funeral. What I didn't tell you is that the elderly gentleman in that story is my dad. If you want to, go back right now and take another look at the picture at the beginning of this section. That's my dad standing between the two sisters. The woman wearing the dark dress on the left is my mom. She was the one we'd come to bury that day.

Dad told me later that when he wrote the letter to the two sisters, he thought my mom's sister (the one on the right, in the light dress) would write him back. She was, after all, the older of the two. But my mom wrote him, so he married her. I told him that I very much appreciated his flexibility.

The way my dad cared for my mom in her last decade of life, and loved her despite her inability to respond to him at any level, was inspiring, heroic, and Christlike. Of the many good gifts God has given to me in my life, surely one of them was the privilege of seeing authentic passion lived out right before my very eyes. When Dad first met that sweet, vibrant girl on the streets of Tallahassee that day, she was beautiful—literally the prom queen of her high school. By the time she died, she was essentially fetal. She couldn't care for herself at all—couldn't feed herself or tend to her own hygiene. She couldn't even turn over in bed. That was, in fact, how he discovered she'd died.

During the last years of Mom's life, Dad would wake up about three times each night, every few hours, and turn her over in her sleep. On their last night together, he awoke to turn her over around 2:00 a.m. and her body was warm. But when he woke to turn her over again about three hours later, her body was cold. That's when he knew she was gone. But he loved her, right down to the last hours of her life. It was, to all of us who knew them, a true love story—a love story of authentic passion.

What animates these final chapters—indeed, this entire book—are two simple facts:

1. All of us want to be loved like that; and
2. All of us *have* been loved like that—even way beyond that.

To use the words of Titus:

At one time we too were foolish, disobedient, deceived and enslaved by all kinds of passions and pleasures. We lived in malice and envy, being hated and hating one another. But when the kindness and love of God our Savior appeared, he saved us, not because of righteous things we had done, but because of his mercy. He saved us through the washing of rebirth and renewal by the Holy Spirit, whom he poured out on us generously through Jesus Christ our Savior, so that, having been justified by his grace, we might become heirs having the hope of eternal life. (Titus 3: 3-7)

If we can communicate to our students these two grand facts in a persuasive way and massage these truths into every nook and cranny of our programs, we'll surely build youth ministries that build passionate disciples. But it won't just happen. Power plants don't just automatically deliver power. It takes a process of careful, prayerful building (chapter 1).

Let's review the key components of such a ministry:

- It all begins in the heart of a passionate leader, just like you, who's experienced that kind of passion and power (chapter 2).
- And because the conductor of this passion and power is relationships, the ministry will focus on helping teenagers connect with parents, peers, and caring adults in ways that nurture and deepen those relationships (chapter 3).
- Through those relationships, that love is channeled into a vision for real-life teenaged disciples: students who are growing into the likeness of Jesus, becoming more mature, being equipped to do the work of ministry, and receiving nurture in the soil of genuine community (chapter 4).
- The vision takes shape in a philosophy of ministry that recognizes that students are at different places on their faith journey, and that incarnational ministry calls us to meet them where they are—no matter where that may be (chapter 5).
- But then, because God is a redeeming God, we intentionally design ministry programs and strategies that don't just leave

them where they are, but instead move them deeper, closer, and further in their intimacy with Christ (chapter 6).

• Those programs and strategies will be diverse enough to meet the needs of different kinds of kids in holistic expressions of Knowing, Doing, and Feeling (chapter 7).

• And all of it will be done with the aim of helping our students become passionate, life-long lovers of Jesus who burn but don't burn out. And we'll do this by offering direction in the road of faith (chapter 8), the tools required for maintaining faith (chapter 9), and the memories that mark the milestones of faith (chapter 10).

Thanks for caring enough to undertake such a grand adventure. It's a high and holy honor to serve with you.

God bless you in this work!

A BRIEF BIBLIOGRAPHY OF SUGGESTED RESOURCES

One of God's gifts to his Church has been the growing wealth of resources for doing thoughtful, creative, and theologically sound youth ministry. A complete and comprehensive bibliography would be huge—too lengthy to offer the kind of "where to start" guidance I intend for the list below. My goal here is simply to suggest a few titles in relevant categories. With that in mind, I've limited my suggestions to books that speak directly to the topics addressed in this book. Think of this list as an appetizer. Thanks to various online sites (YouthSpecialties.com, SimplyYouthMinistry.com, NavPress.com), there are lots of ways to sample the full buffet.

ADOLESCENT SPIRITUALITY

Clark, Chap. *Hurt: Inside the World of Today's Teenagers*. Grand Rapids, MI: Baker Academic, 2004.

Dean, Kenda Creasy. *Almost Christian: What the Faith of Our Teenagers is Telling the American Church*. New York: Oxford University Press, 2010.

Robbins, Duffy. *This Way to Youth Ministry: An Introduction to the Adventure*. Grand Rapids, MI: Youth Specialties/Zondervan, 2004. See especially chapter 11.

Smith, Christian, and Melinda Lundquist Denton. *Soul Searching: The Religious and Spiritual Lives of American Teenagers*. New York: Oxford University Press, 2005.

EXPERIENTIAL YOUTH MINISTRY

Losey, John. *Experiential Youth Ministry Handbook: How Intentional Activity Can Make the Spiritual Stuff Stick.* Grand Rapids, MI: Youth Specialties/Zondervan, 2004.

Losey, John, *Experiential Youth Ministry Handbook, Volume 2: Using Intentional Activity to Grow the Whole Person.* Grand Rapids, MI: Youth Specialties/Zondervan, 2007.

WEB-BASED RESOURCES FOR MULTISENSORY WORSHIP

http://experientialworship.com: An excellent site with myriad resources

www.ionabooks.com: Ancient rituals and liturgy for contemporary worship

www.taize.fr: Resources for contemplative worship

www.eyeeffectsworship.com: Visual images for worship

www.radiatefilms.com: Still and video backgrounds for worship

www.worshipfilms.com: Devotional videos for worship

www.highwaymedia.org: Creative videos for worship

PROGRAMMING FOR DISCIPLESHIP

Fields, Doug. *Purpose-Driven Youth Ministry.* Grand Rapids, MI: Youth Specialties/Zondervan, 1998.

Julian, Kent. *101 Ideas for Making Disciples in Your Youth Group.* Grand Rapids, MI: Youth Specialties/Zondervan, 2008.

Powell, Kara E., Brad M. Griffin, and Cheryl A. Crawford. *Sticky Faith, Youth Worker Edition: Practical Ideas to Nurture Long-Term Faith in Teenagers.* Grand Rapids, MI: Youth Specialties/Zondervan, 2011.

Robbins, Duffy. *The Ministry of Nurture: A Youth Worker's Guide to Discipling Teenagers.* Grand Rapids, MI: Youth Specialties/Zondervan, 1990.

Thomas, Gary. *Sacred Pathways: Discover Your Soul's Path to God*. Revised Edition. Grand Rapids, MI: Zondervan, 2010.

TOOLS OF DISCIPLE-MAKING

Acts of Mercy/Service

Claiborne, Shane. *The Irresistible Revolution: Living as an Ordinary Radical*. Grand Rapids, MI: Zondervan, 2006.

Bible Study

Fields, Doug. *Refuel: An Uncomplicated Guide to Connecting with God*. Nashville, TN: Thomas Nelson, 2008.

Lambert, Dan. *Teaching That Makes a Difference: How to Teach for Holistic Impact*. Grand Rapids, MI: Youth Specialties/Zondervan, 2004. See especially "The World's Longest List of Teaching Methods" (there are 217 of them with examples for each).

Shafer, Barry. *Unleashing God's Word in Youth Ministry*. Grand Rapids, MI: Youth Specialties/Zondervan, 2008.

Shafer, Barry. *See, Believe, Live: An Inductive Study in John (Digging Deeper)*. Grand Rapids, MI: Youth Specialties/Zondervan, 2008.

Prayer

Foster, Richard J. *Celebration of Discipline: The Path to Spiritual Growth*. San Francisco: Harper, 1978.

Yaconelli, Mark. *Downtime: Helping Teenagers Pray*. Grand Rapids, MI: Youth Specialties/Zondervan, 2008.

Meditation/Contemplation

Kimball, Dan, and Lilly Lewin. *Sacred Space: A Hands-On Guide to Creating Multisensory Worship Experiences for Youth Ministry*. Grand Rapids, MI: Youth Specialties/Zondervan, 2008.

Robbins, Maggie, and Duffy Robbins. *Enjoy the Silence: A 30-Day Experiment in Listening to God*. Grand Rapids, MI: Youth Specialties/Zondervan, 2005.

Yaconelli, Mark. *Contemplative Youth Ministry: Practicing the Presence of Jesus.* Grand Rapids, MI: Youth Specialties/Zondervan, 2006.

Yaconelli, Mark. *Growing Souls: Experiments in Contemplative Youth Ministry.* Grand Rapids, MI: Youth Specialties/Zondervan, 2007.

MEMORY-MAKING

Fields, Doug, and Duffy Robbins. *Memory Makers.* Grand Rapids, MI: Youth Specialties/Zondervan, 1996.

BOOKS THAT HAVE FORMED MY UNDERSTANDING OF DISCIPLESHIP

Anderson, Keith R., and Randy D. Reese. *Spiritual Mentoring: A Guide for Seeking and Giving Direction.* Downers Grove, IL: InterVarsity, 1999.

Bonhoeffer, Dietrich. *The Cost of Discipleship.* Translated by R. H. Fuller. New York: MacMillan, 1963.

Coleman, Robert E. *The Master Plan of Evangelism.* Grand Rapids, MI: Revell Books, 2006.

Eims, LeRoy. *The Lost Art of Disciple Making.* Grand Rapids, MI: Zondervan, 1978.

Moore, Waylon B. *Multiplying Disciples: The New Testament Method for Church Growth.* Colorado Springs, CO: Navpress, 1981.

Peterson, Eugene H. *A Long Obedience in the Same Direction: Discipleship in an Instant Society* Downers Grove, IL: InterVarsity Press, 1980.

Trotman, Dawson. *Born to Reproduce.* Colorado Springs, CO: Navpress, 1981.

Wilkins, Michael J. *Following the Master: Discipleship in the Steps of Jesus.* Grand Rapids, MI: Zondervan, 1992.

Speaking to Teenagers

How to Think About, Create, and Deliver Effective Messages

Doug Fields and Duffy Robbins

Get ready for a crash course in effective communication. More than just a book on how to "do talks," *Speaking to Teenagers* combines the experience and wisdom of two veteran youth ministry speakers, along with insightful research and practical tools, to help you develop messages that engage students with the love of Christ and the power of his Word.

Whether you're crafting a five-minute devotional or a 30-minute sermon, *Speaking to Teenagers* is essential to understanding and preparing great messages.

Together, Doug Fields and Duffy Robbins show you how they craft their own messages and give you the tools to do it yourself. They'll guide you, step-by-step, through the process of preparing and delivering meaningful messages that effectively communicate to your students.

Fields and Robbins walk you through three dimensions of a message—he speaker, the listener, and the message itself—and introduce you to the concept and principles of inductive communication. You'll also get helpful tips on finding illustrations for your talk and using them for maximum impact, as well as insights on reading your audience and effective body language.

As *Speaking to Teenagers* guides you toward becoming a more effective communicator, you'll find that this book·s practical principles will positively impact the way you view, treat, and communicate to teenagers.

Available in stores and online!

Youth Ministry Nuts and Bolts, Revised and Updated

Organizing, Leading, and Managing Your Youth Ministry

Duffy Robbins

Youth ministry veteran and bestselling author, Duffy Robbins, offers an updated and revised edition of his book about the important, behind-the-scenes mechanics of youth ministry. The tasks of budgeting, decision-making, time management, team ministry, staff relationships, conflict resolution, working with parents, and a range of other issues, are the things that keep a ministry together and functioning well. Nobody gets into youth ministry because they want to think about these things; but a lot of people get out of youth ministry because they didn't think about them. All youth workers—whether paid or volunteer, full-time or part-time—will find *Youth Ministry Nuts and Bolts* to be a thoughtful, fun, practical guide to youth ministry administration.

Available in stores and online!

Share Your Thoughts

With the Author: Your comments will be forwarded to the author when you send them to *zauthor@zondervan.com*.

With Zondervan: Submit your review of this book by writing to *zreview@zondervan.com*.

Free Online Resources at

www.zondervan.com

Zondervan AuthorTracker: Be notified whenever your favorite authors publish new books, go on tour, or post an update about what's happening in their lives at www.zondervan.com/authortracker.

Daily Bible Verses and Devotions: Enrich your life with daily Bible verses or devotions that help you start every morning focused on God. Visit www.zondervan.com/newsletters.

Free Email Publications: Sign up for newsletters on Christian living, academic resources, church ministry, fiction, children's resources, and more. Visit www.zondervan.com/newsletters.

Zondervan Bible Search: Find and compare Bible passages in a variety of translations at www.zondervanbiblesearch.com.

Other Benefits: Register yourself to receive online benefits like coupons and special offers, or to participate in research.